ALWAYS CHASE THE LIGHT

JENNIFER N. GEEN

GRAYLIGHT COLLECTIVE

SAINT LOUIS

Always Chase the Light
Jennifer N. Geen

Published by Graylight Collective, St. Louis, MO

Limit of Liability/Disclaimer of Warranty: While the publisher and author have used their best efforts in preparing this book, they make no representations or warranties with respect to the accuracy or completeness of the contents of this book and specifically disclaim any implied warranties of merchantability or fitness for a particular purpose. No warranty may be created or extended by sales representatives or written sales materials. The advice and strategies contained herein may not be suitable for your situation. You should consult with a professional where appropriate. Neither the publisher nor the author shall be liable for any loss of profit or any other commercial damages, including but not limited to special, incidental, consequential, or other damages.

The product information and advice provided (in this book) are intended for general informational purposes only. The author and publisher of this book have made every effort to ensure that the content is accurate and up-to-date at the time of publication. However, they make no representations or warranties of any kind, express or implied, about the completeness, accuracy, reliability, suitability, or availability of the information, products, or services contained in this book for any purpose.

Project Management and Book Design: DavisCreativePublishing.com

Library of Congress Cataloging-in-Publication Data

Names: Geen, Jennifer N., author.
Title: Always chase the light / Jennifer N. Geen.
Description: Saint Louis : Graylight Collective, [2025]
Identifiers: LCCN: 2025920347 | ISBN: 9798998905414 (paperback) | 9798998905421 (ebook)
Subjects: LCSH: Cancer--Patients--Family relationships. | Parents of cancer patients--Psychology. | Mothers and sons. | Perseverance (Ethics) | Resilience (Personality trait) | Faith. | BISAC: BODY, MIND & SPIRIT / General. | MEDICAL / Oncology / Pediatric. | RELIGION / Faith.
Classification: LCC: RC262 .G44 2025 | DDC: 362.196994--dc23

Do not be overtaken by darkness.

Find the light.
Be the light.

For Oliver,
the light of my life and
for my mom Colleen,
whose light shines through me

CONTENTS

PROLOGUE

It was a bright and chilly January morning, exactly 9:58 a.m., as we walked into the Color Tex Studio C. My first time in a professional photography/videography studio since I had my senior pictures taken twenty years ago, in the summer of 2001.

It was a large warehouse-type space that was split into distinct sections for different scenes. A kitchen, a living room, and a space that was completely a blank slate, all white floor and walls. Ollie would be positioned for his photos in the blank slate area. It was pristine, with racks of all sorts of props of different clothes, wigs, and accessories off to the side.

The photographer had his gear set up with large television screens set vertically on moveable racks to preview the photos in real time as he shot them. He was taking some test photos, testing the light. The flash was bright against the white walls and floor. The click of his camera was loud in the quiet stillness of the space. Ollie seemed excited and happy. He was on the brink of turning four and wanted to run around and be silly.

As we left our home that morning, I told Ollie we were working on another "special project" together. He was agreeable, and I was excited that our family had been asked to help the local Chapter of a national not-for-profit organization. This particular organization directly benefited the two hospitals that helped save Ollie's precious life.

Our plate had been full of both large and small asks from various philanthropic organizations, but giving our time and sharing Ollie's story was the very least we felt like we could do.

A few weeks prior, we had helped the Cardinal Glennon Foundation with a film project. I assumed the project was to be filmed by cell phones to post on their website or social media sites. A quick in and out, and nothing too fancy. They had told us it was a "special project" and to wear certain colors of comfortable clothes, but that was it. To the contrary, it was the exact opposite. Elaborate and facilitated by a professional film crew in town from Los Angeles, California.

There was some secrecy around that film project, and we didn't have a lot of details other than it could be related to the rumor of a new Cardinal Glennon Children's Hospital being built. Another experience that felt absolutely out of body. That film ended up being a commercial featuring Ollie and me, along with others, that was broadcast on local television (TV) for several months.

To be honest, throughout this whole ordeal, there were just so many things, people, and events that I could have never in a million years predicted we would be a part of, both good and bad. One thing I knew for sure was that I felt called to be a conduit to help support the institutions that helped us, and there were so many. The past eighteen months had been much of a blur. Surreal in most ways. In fact, the experience still feels that way. I think it will forever.

Today was a kickoff photoshoot for the Children's Miracle Network of Greater St. Louis. Ollie was asked to be one of four Ambassador Children for the region. Each year, two children are selected from Cardinal Glennon Children's Hospital and two children from the Children's Hospital. The organization directly raises money for both healthcare institutions and splits it on research, technological advances, Child Life, and family services. But before we get to that, we need to start at the beginning.

How did we get here? I'll start with the day that our lives changed forever: Friday, October 23, 2021.

CHAPTER 1

SUNSET

October 23, 2021:

It was a late fall afternoon when I picked Ollie up from his Montessori school, Lakeside Children's Academy. Weather wise, it was such a pleasant day, in the mid-sixties. The sun was just beginning to transition to dusk. Ollie asked if we could stop at a playground on our way home. He often asked if we could stop and play on the way home, and that was something I really enjoyed doing with him at the end of my workday. He seemed to be in a joyful and playful mood, and I remember being relieved and happy about his disposition.

It had been a tough couple of weeks of temperamental moods for our two-year-old. But he was our only child, and as first-time parents, we thought it was just normal toddler behavior; working through expressing himself and his emotions, not having the words to communicate fully just yet. So, naturally, I said an enthusiastic "yes" to his question about playing at the park. "That will be a fun way to kick off our weekend," I said aloud and smiled as I looked at him in the rearview mirror.

We drove to Des Peres Park, a beautiful suburban St. Louis County Park, a short ten minutes from his school. Des Peres Park was a favorite as it is a large park with many amenities, including: not one, but two playgrounds—one for younger children and one for older kids; a walking trail; a lake with a pedestrian bridge, friendly ducks, and geese; baseball fields and tennis and pickleball courts.

We easily found a parking spot, and I got out and walked around the car and unbuckled Ollie from his car seat. I lifted him out of his seat, set him on the pavement, and we walked up to the path joyfully holding hands. Then he saw the playgrounds and took off running, so excited to play. It made me smile and chuckle. Then, as he was about five feet in front of me, he lost his footing and fell face down on his belly.

Running now too, I scooped him up and took a seat on a half wall that was a few feet ahead of us and next to the big kids' playground. I held him close to console him. He was very upset, tears streaming down his face.

Thankfully, Ollie had on a sweatsuit, and I took a quick look to see if he had any scrapes or bruises, but thankfully, he didn't. It was a strange fall. As a toddler, he really didn't trip much, so this awkward fall definitely surprised me. It was a literal face plant. It looked like it hurt, but yet, no blood. I was perplexed, and Ollie was inconsolable.

I asked him if he was okay and if he wanted to stay and play. He said, through his tears, he wanted to "go home." This seemed odd to me, especially since I didn't see anything visibly wrong with him. So, I gave it a few minutes. We sat there together on that brick wall. I held him, and he was clearly not calming down. He kept repeating one thing, over and over, "My belly hurts." I decided we needed to go, and as I was walking him back to the car, I thought maybe he'd had the wind knocked out of him and he was startled by it. I remembered that happening to me as a kid and how confusing and shocking it was.

He stopped crying only once while I got him buckled into his car seat. I promptly turned his kids' music on, hoping it would help settle him, but the look of sadness took over his face. He looked absolutely miserable. I kept verbally and visually checking in on him in the rearview mirror. I distinctly remember thinking the situation was odd, that something just didn't seem right. That escalated. He didn't talk or really move on the twenty-minute drive home. This was normally a kid who didn't stop talking. I thought to myself that he really didn't look like he felt good. I called my husband Brian and told him what had happened, and said, "Maybe he has the flu or COVID." I was perplexed.

After his crying subsided, besides being generally lethargic, you wouldn't have thought twice about the toddler fall. We lay on the sofa together, snuggling closely. I thought he was tired from daycare. I thought he could be coming down with a sickness like the flu. Typical mom worries. After all, we had so far managed to dodge the ever-evolving pandemic virus for eighteen months.

I gave him some kids' Motrin, put him to bed a little early to get some extra rest, and Brian and I enjoyed the remainder of our Friday evening with some wine, burgers on the grill, and an episode of our favorite TV show.

On Saturday morning, Ollie seemed to wake up feeling normal-ish. He slept through the night and woke up ready to eat breakfast and play.

We eventually got ready to head out to our first park of the day. We joked with friends that Ollie was the "park connoisseur" because on the weekends, we often frequented at least two, sometimes three parks a day. The plan for this day was no different. The weather was perfect for getting out and about in nature.

The onset of the pandemic in March of 2020, just after Ollie's first birthday, had changed daily life in a lot of ways for most people. In 2021, a vaccine for children under five had not yet been approved. With a small child who was still not able to be vaccinated and who was unwilling to wear a mask in public spaces, the situation left us with few indoor options if we planned on playing it safe. So, we opted for mostly outdoor activities and experiences, and local parks were a great fit for our family time.

However, that morning, after breakfast, trying to get him out the door involved several asks to "get shoes on." Did he hear us? Was he ignoring us? Did he not want to go? I noticed he was operating a little slower than normal and with less enthusiasm. I was sitting cross-legged on the floor, and he finally came over and sat on my lap. However, as he sat down, he leaned back into me. In that moment, I swore, it looked and felt like his eyes rolled into the back of his head and like he was going to pass out. It was such a brief but strange and startling experience. I actually thought maybe I had imagined it.

I called for Brian to see if he had seen it too, but he was already outside in the garage, in the car, waiting for us. So, in a bit of a panicked voice, I asked Ollie if he was okay, and he said "Yes," so we got up and out we went.

Looking back on the pictures from that morning, so much more makes sense now. His skin coloring was grayish. He was a bit lethargic. He had that moment of looking like he might pass out. Cobbled together those things might indicate something was wrong. But in the moment, we were just living.

When we got to the park, he played on the merry-go-round, swings, and slides. I remember it vividly; the weather that day, the drive to the park, the place we picked, a small neighborhood park in Webster Groves. One we had never been to before.

The following day, late Sunday morning and early afternoon, we went to a local pumpkin patch with Brian's parents, my in-laws, Jerry and Anna Geen. We were all so excited for him to experience the magic of the Halloween season. But just about the entire time we were at the Pumpkin Patch, he was unhappy. He didn't even want to jump in the bounce houses. He just wanted to be held by me. I was frustrated but also concerned. Something still seemed a bit off.

Sunday went on, and in the late afternoon I had a call, a *FaceTime* video chat with four of my best friends from high school who all lived in different states: Angie, Alissa, Lisa, and Shannon. We had started this tradition recently, as the pandemic loomed on. It was an opportunity to check in with each other. To laugh, support, lament, remember, and connect. A fun social activity during a strange time when we couldn't physically be together. It was truly a highlight of my day.

We strategically planned our calls during nap time, as a few of us had young ones. I told my friends how Ollie had been cranky lately, fell at the playground, and had said his belly hurt. In general, I explained that he had been acting a bit "off" all weekend.

We talked a bit about the varying pandemic virus mutations that were presenting as gastrointestinal symptoms.

My friend Lisa offered the suggestion of having Ollie tested for COVID before returning to his daycare on Monday.

I thought it was a good idea as he was still complaining that his belly hurt. But I also dreaded making him complete a nose swab to test for this, but knew that it was probably for the best. We all enjoyed our conversation, and as we were wrapping up, I heard Ollie start to wake in his crib upstairs.

I ran up the stairs, happy to see him. When I picked him up, his clothes were drenched in sweat. His little face was damp and red. He was cranky, unhappy, and clearly uncomfortable. The most discomfort he had been in since Friday. I had this innate sense that we needed to go to urgent care immediately to figure out what was going on with this bellyache.

I was scared that he actually did have COVID. The virus and how it presented were still very uncertain, and new mutations were popping up each week.

I told Brian I would make an appointment for the next available time at an urgent care clinic down the street. Urgent care on Sunday evening never sounds great, but at least we would have some answers and be able to get our boy help in feeling better. And if he was contagious, we didn't want to send him back to school in the morning.

However, nothing could have ever prepared us for what was to come over the following 48 hours.

Within the plethora of urgent care facilities, we were fortunate enough to live by two that specialized in children's care. The first one that came to mind was St. Louis Children's, an after-hours clinic located in a strip mall about a mile from our home. I was familiar with it as it was adjacent to my fitness studio, Orangetheory.

During the height of the pandemic, my fellow workout friends and I were not allowed to congregate in the Orangetheory studio lobby before class, so we would have to stand outside in a line.

We would be masked up, awkwardly talking, shivering because it was well before the sun came up, and looking around at our surroundings.

I often peeked into the twenty-four-hour children's clinic while waiting, thinking about the kids and families I'd see inside in the small waiting room.

It's never fun to be sick, and the added layer of stress from the ongoing pandemic made most people in general feel extra tense and fearful. Especially people with kids. I noticed that the facility was often quite busy.

I made an online appointment for Ollie for 5 p.m. We walked out of our home, got into our car, and started the short drive up to the shopping plaza. In less than five minutes we would be there.

We parked, got out of the vehicle, and approached the door of the clinic. However, when I pulled the handle to open the door, it was locked. It was then that I saw a small sign on the door that said to call a specific number to let the receptionist know you had arrived for your appointment.

So, I called the number and gave Ollie's name and date of birth. The receptionist paused and asked me which location I had made the appointment at. I repeated the location, but she said she couldn't find him in the system. She went on to say that they couldn't see him now and were completely booked until later that evening. We then walked back to our parked car, holding Ollie, standing in the brisk air of the fall evening. Brian and I were frustrated and tired. We debated on what to do. Wait? Go to a different location? Go home? And just then, I remembered there was a brand-new Cardinal Glennon urgent care facility about a mile and a half from where we were standing.

However, I wasn't sure if it was open yet, as it was just recently under construction. We decided to Google it and call and check.

Our phone call was answered, and the receptionist let us know that yes, they were open and there was no wait. Thank God!

Relieved, we got into the car and made our way south down Tesson Ferry Road about five minutes from where we were parked. The sun was setting as we pulled into the parking lot. The lot was freshly paved and only had a few cars in it, likely the employees. We approached the glass door entryway and went in.

The facility was sparkling clean with a "new smell" of sorts. An empty waiting room, with a number of televisions with cartoons on. We felt like the experience would go as well as it could. Hopefully, we would be in and out within an hour or so. Maybe this was the flu, COVID, or some other gastrointestinal issue. We had been lucky that

Ollie hadn't really had a lot of health issues in his short two years of life outside of ear infections. We would get a diagnosis, some medicine, and get home in time for our bedtime routine.

I took a seat to complete his initial intake paperwork, then I walked the clipboard and stack of papers back up to the reception desk, and returned to my seat. Within a few minutes, we were called back to the examination area. Height, weight, and vitals such as temperature, blood pressure, and blood oxygen percentages were all taken in a small area directly off to the right of the entry hallway. Ollie did so great for a kid who had never done these tests.

The nurse took off the tiny blood pressure cuff, wrapped it up, and said, "Everything looks good," which left me a bit perplexed, as I was convinced that his vitals would give some indication of sickness, a fever, or something. She then walked us back to an exam room and closed the door. The spaces were brand new. Like we could have been one of the very first occupants in that exam room.

We waited and waited. It seemed like a long time, but it was probably only fifteen minutes or so.

Those small, windowless, quiet, cold rooms always make the concept of time seem slow. We were also anxious.

The door opened. "Hi, I'm Jenny." Nurse Practitioner Jenny had just introduced herself. She came into the room with a big, kind-hearted smile and a bubbly demeanor. While we couldn't actually see our smiles because we all had masks on, you could tell when someone was smiling based on how their eyes looked above the mask. I was instantly relieved we had been connected with a human who seemed genuinely happy to be at her job.

Jenny was thoughtful and thorough. She went through all the introductory questions and seemed to be concerned: "What brought us here today? What's been going on?"

As she started to examine Ollie, we told her about the fall at the playground on Friday, just two days earlier, and tried our best to explain we didn't seem overly concerned.

Racking my brain, I then added, "Maybe he cracked a rib with the fall?"

I went through the replay in my mind of his fall. I was grasping, throwing out any possible thing it could be. I wanted answers.

I would have thought Ollie would be in more pain if he had actually cracked a rib, but you just never know. What could possibly be causing this belly pain? Was he constipated?

They started with a COVID and a flu test, both of which required the giant nose swabs. As expected, that didn't go over well. Poor kid. Both tests came back negative, which was somewhat of a relief, but also confusing. Jenny looked at Ollie's belly, pressing on it a bit. Noting to us that it felt "hard." She asked about his bowel movements and how he had been eating.

We didn't think or notice anything that was "abnormal"—he was doing both; eating and pooping. She then ordered an x-ray. Ollie and I held hands as they walked us down the long hallway into the very large x-ray room.

The room was dark and loud with lights glowing in the dimness. After asking me if I could be pregnant, to which I replied, "No," they gave me the heavy apron protector to cover my abdomen and started the series of photographs.

Ollie did exceptional, both timid and overwhelmed. He was quiet and very still as he held my hand. I talked him through what they were doing, "seeing inside his belly." He complied with their requests to stand in certain positions. First front-facing, then to each side.

With my focus on my son's mental and physical comfort, I didn't think twice about the x-rays. I thought that they must be checking for a cracked rib, like I had mentioned. At this point, I truly wasn't overly alarmed or concerned, thinking soon we would know what was going on with him so that we could help him feel better.

Ollie and I kept our hands locked together as we exited the x-ray room and walked back to the exam room.

We sat back down, waiting for what we presumed would be some sort of news.

Jenny came back in with her hypothesis. Ollie could be constipated. They offered us an enema or a MiraLAX drink to "get things moving."

We decided to take the faster of the available options to get Ollie some relief from this "bellyache." We felt bad that he had been in discomfort, for what we assumed was most of the weekend.

Jenny assisted with the task of inserting the enema, and our family of three made our way to the restroom.

We helped Ollie onto the big potty, he was just two, and held his hand as he cried. We had just started potty training after all, but on a small training potty. He was confused, probably scared, angry, and annoyed from being poked and prodded. He didn't want to try to go poop on a big potty.

It was loud in the bathroom from his cry echoing. All we could do was try our best to remain calm and reassure Ollie that he would feel better soon. I took a deep breath and encouraged Ollie to do so as well, as the sound continued to amplify in the small space. More deep breaths. We tried to rationally talk our son through the mission–getting the poop out. If you are a parent, you will understand this whole charade. We waited it out, but nothing. Nothing came out.

I was concerned, confused, and vocal. Wasn't this like a "sure thing" to get it out? I had no experience with enemas. We eventually made our way back to the exam room. Jenny came back in, and I told her he didn't get anything out. She said that for some people, it just takes longer.

We were discharged with a prescription for the milder laxative, MiraLAX.

Leaving the urgent care, we were relieved in some ways, thinking Ollie's belly hurt due only to constipation–what we thought was a relatively easy fix.

A normal type of diagnosis. Better than the flu and/or COVID, I thought.

After a quick stop at the pharmacy, we made it home and went about our evening routine. Cooked a quick dinner. A bath for Ollie. We read books, and then it was time for bed. I checked in several times on Ollie's diaper situation throughout the night—concerned he would have leakage, but still nothing?

In my mind's eye, the thought emoji appeared. "*Hmmm*," I thought. "*Will it work?*" We will just keep him home from school tomorrow to be safe. Soon, this will all pass. No big deal.

Ollie was tucked into his crib by 9 p.m. Brian and I slept hard after the intensity of the evening, and by all accounts, thought nothing out of the ordinary about the urgent care visit.

CHAPTER 2

DARKNESS

It would be haunting hindsight, in the coming months, that would help me make some sense of the unimaginable. It was, however, leading me down the rabbit holes and traps of: "Why didn't we ask more questions?" or "insist on more tests" or "realize that something wasn't right." In hindsight, it is so easy to blame yourself. That is natural. My best advice is that if something doesn't seem right, it probably isn't.

You and only you will be the best advocate for yourself and your kids. I say this because we did ask Ollie's pediatrician at his two-year checkup in January 2021 about his belly. He thought it looked normal. We asked him because Ollie's belly was visibly distended, nothing terrible, but definitely rounded and noticeable. We thought it was a toddler belly.

I tried to give myself some grace as a first-time parent. There was no way of knowing what was to come for Ollie, but I instinctively felt guilty. I was responsible for him and was devastated that we had not noticed small signs along the way, that there may have been a problem.

I was the parent. I was supposed to be the ultimate protector. But truthfully, there was no way to know. And that's why I believe that the fall Ollie experienced so randomly and dramatically was a form of divine intervention. A way for us to get him help before it was too late. I feel strongly as though the fall saved his precious life. Something so simple, yet mind-blowing. Had he not fallen directly on his belly that day at the park, when would we have found out? Weeks or months later? Lots of "what ifs".

It was Monday morning, October 25th, what seemed to be a normal day. We got up as we always do, had our coffee and breakfast, and got ready for work. We were trying to figure out how to juggle caring for Ollie for the day, as he was going to need to be home from daycare. We had given him all those laxatives–yet, still nothing. I recall thinking that was odd. But moved on. Everyone is different, so maybe it was just taking longer than expected, as Jenny has noted.

At this time, life moved at a pace that was like a freight train with no destination.

We were on an autopilot of sorts. We were still in a season of learning how to best manage our lives as working parents in demanding roles. We had some experience with juggling schedules because of the isolation requirements of the pandemic, which had been ongoing now for over a year.

First, we had been at home quarantined for months, and then once Ollie finally was able to return to daycare, the facility would get shut down for a week if there was a positive COVID case. Due to the ever-evolving mutations and recommendations from the CDC and local authorities, protocols were fluid. It can't be overstated just how much of an uncertain and difficult time the pandemic was for everyone.

Especially people in vulnerable populations: young, old, sick, and/or immunocompromised. This day, it was determined that I would take the morning shift with Ollie, 8 a.m. to noon, as Brian had some meetings he simply couldn't clear last minute.

I prepared Ollie's breakfast and set up the living room with toys, a movie, and some additional snacks. I put in my wireless headphones and called into my 8:30 a.m. Microsoft Teams meeting on my iPhone, coming off mute only when I needed to respond to a question.

I grabbed my second cup of coffee.

I greeted a service worker who was scheduled to come and finish our new HVAC installation. He had been troubleshooting our new wi-fi thermostat integration. Sometime around 9:30 a.m., I got a call from a number I was unfamiliar with. I decided to answer it instead of letting it go to voicemail. I don't usually do that but thank goodness I did.

It was a gentleman, I don't remember his name, although I'm sure he said it. He was calling from Cardinal Glennon Children's Hospital.

I thought instantly, "Oh, this is a survey or something, as a follow-up to our urgent care visit yesterday." It seems like there are constantly follow-up surveys these days.

I knew it was a good thing, but generally I didn't choose to participate.

Oh, how I wish that was simply what the call was about. It was not a survey. It was very serious.

The man was calling as a follow-up to our urgent care visit, but he had news. Completely unexpected, earth-shattering news.

The man said to me, "The radiologist has reviewed Ollie's x-rays and found a mass." I could immediately feel my heart start to beat fast with anxiety. Then it felt like my stomach was sucker punched. He said, "You need to come to the hospital's emergency room, right away, and pack an overnight bag."

Wait! What? "A mass?"

I blinked hard. My heart now felt like it was literally outside of my body.

I asked, "What do you mean by a mass?" He explained he couldn't say more at this time, but that we needed to get to the hospital as soon as possible. I asked him to clarify if in a few hours was fine, and he said "No, *as soon as possible*. Do not wait. Pack up your bag and come now."

It was a call I will never forget. I hung up, and I was quivering. I was confused. I was in the early stages of panic.

I took as deep a breath as I could, and I called Brian, but my voice was shaking and I was speaking fast, as I thought about exactly how I was going to tell him this news. The phone rang a few times, then he picked up. "Brian, you need to come home as soon as possible so we can take Ollie to Cardinal Glennon Hospital. They just called, and the radiologist who reviewed his x-ray from last night found something, a mass…"

I could hardly say it out loud.

I was trying so hard to keep it together, but the fear was creeping in, minute by minute.

I told our service worker, who had overheard most of this conversation, that we had just got a call to go to the emergency room (ER), but that he could keep working.

Even though I was scared and startled, I didn't really think we would actually need that overnight bag the employee referenced; we would surely be home in a few hours. After all, it was still the morning. All day at the hospital? How? It truly seemed impossible that we would be there over twelve hours and not be able to be home in our own beds by 9 or 10 p.m.

I recall trying to process the message and reason with it. Like I had some control over it. Of course I didn't. It was what it was.

Ok, an "overnight bag." I ran up the staircase to our room and hastily packed what I thought to be our "essentials", as well as Ollie's. A change of comfortable clothes, pajamas, toothbrushes, and toothpaste; a blanket and stuffies for Ollie; and his sound machine all fit into my favorite vibrant, floral Vera Bradley bag. I zipped it up, and my heart and mind were now in sync and in a full-on panic mode. Thoughts kept racing through my mind, so much so that it was hard to think, but instinctively, I knew I had to appear as calm as I could for Ollie. Not be scared or shaken. After all, we didn't even know what this was all about yet.

What a strange situation.

I truly thought we were just dealing with constipation. Now I'd been directed to come to the hospital as soon as possible. Maybe at this moment, some possible diagnosis could have come to mind, but I was in a state of panic and shock.

I was just going through the motions of what was required to get us there as quickly as we could. I inherently knew that if we got a call like this, something was definitely wrong. But what?

The drive to the hospital was just over ten miles, but that day it seemed like one hundred. Brian drove us and was on repeat, asking me, "What did they say, exactly?"

I repeated what I heard, over and over, replaying it in my mind, word for word, and we sat, stunned. Silent. As if some answer would magically appear.

Brian dropped Ollie and me off at the emergency entrance. The automatic doors opened as we approached. I carried him in, and I took a big breath as I got in line for the registration desk, feet from the entry doors and security module.

To our surprise, registration had a file ready for him, with a hospital identification (ID) bracelet printed out. "Please put this on" and "take a seat" were what we were told after the formalities of identification, insurance paperwork, a signature, and other formal paperwork were completed.

A hospital bracelet? Odd, I thought to myself. I honestly couldn't believe they had all this ready for us. We had just received the call to come in about sixty minutes prior. They were so prepared. I wasn't connecting the dots that he would have a hospital bracelet if he was to be admitted to the hospital, which is why they asked us to "pack a bag."

So, we waited. It was not long before we were called back, maybe a total of fifteen minutes or so. With the push of a button, the big blue double doors opened to the emergency treatment area. The nurse called his name, "Oliver Geen," and with that, Brian, Ollie, and I entered a whole new world that was to be upon us. It felt surreal. It felt scary. It felt out of body.

CHAPTER 3

THE BLACKOUT

The flurry of the ER was astounding, and I was surprised by just how many rooms and people were in this area, especially for first thing on a Monday morning. I had little to no perspective, though, only having been to the ER less than a handful of times in my entire thirty-seven-year-old life.

The room they brought us to was large. In fact, it looked like it could be a surgical suite. I recall thinking that was strange. Lots of overhead lights, an electronic bed in the middle. A wall of supply cabinets and machinery. It was definitely not your standard exam room with a hard medical bed against the wall and two chairs where they check your heart rate, blood pressure, and other vitals. Upon entering, I noticed that thankfully, there were three chairs, not just two, which is what we sat on. One for each of us. We had Ollie take the middle seat.

Sitting down, we were reluctant, as our nerves and anxiety were high, only to get higher and higher with each passing hour we spent in that room. Not much of a choice, though, whether we chose to stand or sit, we were going to be in that room if we liked it or not.

The nurses quickly came in and introduced themselves. I remember they were both so calm and kind. They explained that they needed to prep Ollie for a variety of tests. I know now, they were prepping us, too. An intravenous line (IV) was immediately started through the top of his little hand, which was startling, but obviously necessary. They needed that line to draw blood, they explained. I hadn't mentally prepared myself for the thought of what types of tests Ollie would have to go through. There was no time or space in my mind on our short drive to the hospital to even think for a minute about what might happen next.

Fascinatingly, they made the IV-line kid-friendly, with a clear plastic cover piece over the insertion that they called a "dog door". Once that was established, the nurses then proceeded to put cute dog stickers on it. They do this to help the kids feel like it's something not so scary, maybe even "fun," but also, so hopefully they won't mess with it and rip it out.

This made me sad. You just never imagine your two-year-old child with an IV access point in their hand.

The blood draw was followed by many different types of scans: computed tomography (CT) scan, magnetic resonance imaging (MRI) scan, and waiting. We were in that room for six-plus hours, which to me felt like the equivalent of six days. The nurses even came back with some substantial new toys for Ollie. I couldn't believe it; a child-size plastic electric guitar and a whole set of space alien figures. I thought the gifts were just too much. Little did I know.

We started pacing, thinking, hoping; Brian and I were both a bit panicked and perplexed. At some point, mid-way through the day, a doctor came in to tell us that what they were seeing was undoubtedly "concerning." It was then that it seemed as if they were giving us small digestible pieces of information.

After the doctor exited the room, I told Brian that I sensed something was really wrong. I told him to try to mentally prepare for bad news. We didn't know yet what that was, but you could just tell by the actions of the medical team that whatever Ollie was facing was not something that was going to allow us to be discharged that day.

More time passed, and then, suddenly, the sliding door slowly opened, and in walked a plethora of people. I'm talking like ten medical professionals. I had never seen so many people at once enter through a door at a hospital. It was that exact moment that I knew something was terribly wrong. My heart dropped. I held my breath. I will never forget it.

We were still there, sitting, all three of us in a row. Ollie was thankfully not paying much attention as he was watching a movie on my phone. Three individuals crouched down—one for each of us. They had tissue boxes.

For Ollie, they brought pop-up books for further distraction.

For Brian and I, one held each of our hands. We were then told that our child's mass was most likely cancer, type not yet confirmed, and that he/we would be admitted to the hospital, indefinitely to investigate, confirm, and start a treatment plan.

It was the worst of the worst.

We sat there with absolute shock and horror. How could this be? Our two-year-old child, our Ollie, had cancer?

What?

How?

Time stopped.

Tears ran down my face and saturated my medical mask, which we were required to wear due to the ongoing pandemic. The mask made me feel like I was suffocating in the moment, but it was really the gravity of the news. The medical professionals remained crouched down and held our hands. I remember feeling paralyzed, like I couldn't move.

I looked down at my child, so innocently sitting next to me, enjoying a movie, and felt the greatest fear and heartbreak imaginable. I remember thinking I shouldn't upset Ollie, so I was trying as hard as I could to not outwardly express my emotions such that he would notice. I didn't want my fear to project onto him. In doing this, it felt like the inside of me evaporated and turned to ash.

Questions immersed my mind. "What type of cancer?" I asked–they said, "We don't want to say until it's fully confirmed." I then followed up with the question, "Is it a blood cancer?" One of the physicians replied, "We think it is a solid tumor, and we need to verify if it is malignant or benign with a biopsy."

The various doctors left after our initial questions, and we had a few minutes just the three of us.

We sat in silence for a moment, staring at the floor. Complete disbelief. Overwhelming sadness. It is truly difficult to articulate just how awful those minutes directly after this news was given to us, really were. Brian stepped out of the room to make a few calls, and then I did. He called his parents, Jerry and Anna. I called my dear friend, Lauren. We had been texting all day, me updating her as I could. Now the phone was ringing, and I was going to have to say this news out loud.

Trying to find the correct words for the situation felt challenging. How could I explain this unbelievable and most shocking turn of events in our lives?

I remember my voice quivering. I remember feeling panicked with a sense of some kind of loss, already. Maybe it was a piece of my heart? I remember immediately feeling confusion and anger, like, "Cancer, you already wrecked me once." Didn't I get some kind of an exemption from dealing with it again?

My beloved mother Colleen had died from stage IV lung cancer in 1999, when I was just fifteen years old. We found out about her diagnosis in March of that year, just six months before she passed away in August. It was a scarring experience, one that I still process the grief from to this day.

Now, my two-year-old child had cancer. Like, how, just how, could I possibly have to endure this pain again? It truly felt impossible in the moment. I knew what I was up against. I knew that it could possibly be fatal.

But here I was, and that is the thing about cancer. It doesn't discriminate. How incredibly naive of me to think that by tragically losing my mom to the disease years ago, it meant that I'd be immune from it now.

Wow. Life, you got me.

Real good.

Could this just be a bad dream?

Why me?

Why Ollie?

Why, why, why?

It didn't matter how many deep breaths I took, or hard blinks of my eyes I made, or touching of objects or walls I tried, this wasn't a dream, or a nightmare. I was not dreaming. This was real. It was truly the most unbelievable of circumstances.

A new reality.

A new life.

There was no taking or leaving it. It just was. We were all going to have to fight to endure it. Hope to make it through it.

I prayed to God. I prayed to my mom.

I needed all the strength I could geat.

I needed to understand why this would happen again, but I also instinctively knew that there was no understanding that would ever come of it. I went round and round in that exact "why" scenario as I did with my mom's passing. It's fishing in a well where there are no fish. No answers will ever be provided as to why. You must accept it, or you will continue to torment yourself.

Then I quickly thought, did I endure my mom's passing to deal with my son's? I was trying to put the puzzle together to make some sense of the pain I felt.

I was so overwhelmed and sad.

Thinking in that moment seemed like a bad idea. I knew that whatever we were about to go through was unfortunately going to be one of the worst experiences of my life.

But I had to show up. I had to be there for my child, for my husband, and for myself. I would have to figure out how to find some semblance of light in this void, the ultimate darkness that I was about to enter.

CHAPTER 4

THE VOID

After those few minutes alone, one of the professionals came back into the room with a wheelchair and positioned it outside the sliding door. They said, "Mom, do you want to sit on the wheelchair and hold Ollie?" As they asked me the question about the wheelchair, they explained that we would be admitted directly to Four North (4N) that night.

We would come to find out 4N was the children's oncology floor. Ollie and I sat in the wheelchair. I didn't want to take a ride in that wheelchair, but I felt like they knew something I didn't.

That chair is probably strategic, because the walk to the 4th floor after hearing some of the most devastating news of your life could be problematic.

You might pass out.

You might run.

I was still one hundred percent stunned.

Everything now was happening so fast, after what felt like a very slow day of tests and waiting in that ER Room. I was absolutely in a daze of sorts. But I do vividly remember a few things.

I remember I held Ollie's little body on my lap, but felt as though I was not alive. An out-of-body feeling where you see yourself, but you are not sure if you are alive or dead.

I remember being wheeled through what we would come to know as the back hallways or "shortcuts" of the hospital. The hallways were super bright with the glare of the LED lights. We passed people walking and the nurses at their various stations, but it was too hard for me to look up, to actually acknowledge anyone or look them in the eye.

When we got to our first room, it was spacious and decorated in what I would characterize as a cheerful island motif.

I ignorantly thought that we would be able to keep some semblance of a schedule. Like a hotel stay.

I remember telling the nurses that Ollie "goes to bed at 7 p.m.". In hindsight, this is quite hilarious.

Obviously, and reasonably, I wasn't grasping reality. I was in denial that we were admitted to the children's cancer ward. I was fiercely trying to control some aspects of this situation, of our life.

If we had to be here, I could make our "space" as comfortable and normal as possible. It was a distraction. The thought of controlling any of it. Also, I wasn't prepared. I hadn't really thought about what I put in our overnight bag, because I didn't think we would be staying overnight.

Also, please note, there is no "normal" in the hospital. Our "new normal" would be incessant beeping machines, people constantly coming in and out of our room, standing bedside on the hard tile floor, looking out the window between the large white wood blinds, searching for the sunrise or sunset, and restarting each day like a groundhog with uncertainty and concern. We would then somehow muster a renewed strength to get up and try to manage it all again. day after day.

The first course of action for Ollie would be a blood transfusion; his red blood cell count was low. We would come to find out that when he had fallen on Friday at the park, his belly actually hurt from his tumor bleeding inside his body. He had lost a lot of blood. This completely freaked me out.

Little did I know, however, that a blood transfusion, of all the tests and procedures he would endure, was easy, and one that would make Ollie feel better quickly. One that he would come to do rather often in this whole ordeal.

As I saw them bring that first blood bag in and hang it high, with the type lettering large and visible, it was hard to process. I don't think I was processing. I was just observing. I was enduring, mentally.

A few short hours before, we were simply dealing with a bellyache due to what we thought was constipation. Now we were on the children's oncology floor, preparing for a blood transfusion and to find out exactly what type of cancer Ollie had.

It was the sheer definition of a crisis in hell.

As we settled in the best we could for the night, I stared at my surroundings. I touched the walls again. I wondered if this was real. How could this be real? My child? Cancer, why do you continue to haunt me? Now I was angry.

The hospital room instantly brought back vivid repressed memories, emotion, and trauma of being at the hospital with my mom at age fifteen, and watching her die of cancer. Hours upon hours spent at St. Mary's Hospital in Duluth. We spent the summer of 1999 keeping my mom company as she was bedridden and eventually moved to hospice. When mom slept, I would often walk the halls of the floor she was on, stopping to get coffee with two creams and two sugars in the family room. The warmth and sweetness of the coffee were physically comforting and something I looked forward to enjoying. The hospital space was cold in many ways. The temperature, the esthetics, the reason we were there. The days dragged on. But it was so important that we were there, even as children.

I then relived the moment the nurses pulled the sheet over her body, the morning she passed. It was August 20, 1999. I was awoken and told that she had passed in the night. Shortly thereafter, my siblings and I gathered in her room and stood in a semi-circle around her body and prayed with a priest. It is something that still brings me to tears. I was scared. I was sad. I would have to figure out how to live through this. It was a lot.

My mind then flashed back to March 1999. Mom had just sat my brother Jon and me down in the smoke-filled living room at our small home on Hiway Lane in International Falls, Minnesota to tell us the news. She said she "needed to talk with us." We knew that she had finally gone to the doctor for her lingering cough, one that seemed like it never got better for years.

I was relieved that she finally decided to go and get it checked out.

We had thought that she had "walking pneumonia," something that wasn't great but certainly curable. That was the diagnosis she had first told us, very casually, sometime in February. We also knew she had to have a follow-up biopsy, but being naive children sheltered from the realities of healthcare lingo, we didn't comprehend what a biopsy was or why she might have to have one. She didn't make a big deal about it either. Keep in mind that in 1999, cell phones with internet capabilities were not yet available, so we were not Googling any terms to better understand things. If we wanted to look up anything on the internet, we had to go to the one shared computer that was in our family office space on a dial-up modem connection. Googling things didn't really happen easily. A foreign concept to most people now.

That March afternoon, in 1999, we had just gotten home from school. Luckily, we were able to walk home from the junior high school after dismissal. We lived about a half a mile from school. Jon was about to finish seventh grade, and I, ninth grade.

The sun was out, the snow was beginning to melt, and the street was wet with puddles. It felt warm compared to the dense cold of winter in Northern Minnesota.

I remember being so happy that spring was on its way soon. I was in a good mood thanks to the sunshine. As we approached, I could see Mom's car in the driveway, which meant that she was home already. That was odd; she usually didn't get home until closer to five. It was 3:30 p.m. She was sitting on our plush green striped sofa in the living room when my brother and I walked in the door. We had no idea what was about to hit us, how our world would change and never be the same.

She looked at us, paused, and took a drag of her cigarette. The cloud of smoke thickened around her. We dropped our book bags on the kitchen floor and walked into the living room; I sat on the maroon-colored glider and stared at her.

That's when she said, "I need to talk with you." She looked very serious. She then proceeded to "The doctors think I have walking pneumonia, but the chest x-ray and biopsy show I also have lung cancer." I sat, quiet. Breathless. Stunned. Scared. In disbelief.

I watched my mom intently.

She was scared too, but was trying hard to put on a brave face for her two young children, for whom she was the primary caregiver. In recalling that conversation, she didn't seem overly anxious, surprised, or upset. Maybe she just knew something was wrong, maybe she had been holding it for a while. Either way, she was stoic. That was totally her, though—the definition of strong.

She was an amazing mother to both Jon and me, but also to my six older siblings, who were all grown and either in college or already married with families of their own.

I can't imagine just how difficult it was that day to sit down and tell her children she had cancer. But she was extraordinarily tough.

There was no doubt about that. She birthed eight children!

She reassured us that she would start treatment immediately, both chemotherapy (chemo) and radiation, and that she would be okay. We would make it through this, just like any other tough time we endured. She really believed it and emulated it.

More importantly, I believed her. She was confident and convincing, like, "Let's just do this treatment. Get it done and move on." I thought that was the plan, and that was how we handled it the first few weeks into our new reality.

While I didn't know much about her prognosis and staging until weeks later, while eavesdropping on a conversation she was having with my sister, I did genuinely think that she would be okay. I never held space at that moment for the fact that one of the outcomes of this could, in fact, be death. We surely didn't talk about it either. I would come to find out that my sister Dawn encouraged her to talk more openly to my younger brother and me about the possibility of death, but she just wouldn't. Not then, not later in the hospital either. I learned the gravity of the situation when I learned what the foreign word "hospice" meant. Not a moment before.

My mother, Colleen, was a devout Catholic, just like her mother, my Grandma Mary. We went to church every single Sunday, whether we were in town or out of town. If we were out of town, we would attend a Catholic church service wherever we were visiting. We attended weekly Adoration of the Eucharist at 6 p.m. on Wednesdays, where we would pray the rosary, kneeling. And we attended mass on each Holy day. Mom was often a reader/lector, walking in with the processional. She would hold the bible up high with pride and conviction, staring at the crucifix as she proceeded with the priest and altar boys down the aisle to the front of the church. She always dressed so elegantly and was absolutely beautiful. Mom loved being a part of the mass, and she was a very good public speaker.

Communicating with conviction and public speaking were skills she instilled in me from a very young age.

I remember her telling me, "You will need to know how to speak in public in your life." Her philosophy was you might as well practice at church. So, we did. Whenever they had a children's mass, Jon would volunteer to serve as an altar boy and I as a lector.

We also had a large Jesus picture in our living room. Behind it were the dry palms from Palm Sunday. Below it on a small table, we had a statue of the Virgin Mary with a rosary and votive candle lights.

The rituals and symbols of faith always had been a large part of my life.

Another example of this was our saint necklace medallions purchased at the tiny church gift shop in the basement corner of Saint Thomas Aquinas Church. We wore them around our necks faithfully. I often had several on one strand. I thought they protected me.

God would be with us. I would pray intently and very specifically every single night, staring at my bedroom ceiling in the dark, talking to God until I fell asleep. Asking him to help her, to help us. I told him I would be extra good and helpful, and we would make it through a tough couple of months. God was with us. I definitely felt him, and he would not fail me. He would make this okay. He knew I needed my mom.

My mom was my everything. My parents had a messy divorce when I was young, just three years old, and I didn't have a close or functioning relationship with my dad. My immediate family unit at that time was my mom and my younger brother Jon. We were the three amigos in our 800 square foot home on Hiway Lane. I have so many amazing memories of all the fun we would have—especially playing Scrabble on the large woven oval rug in our living room on Saturday evenings, listening to music on our six-disc CD changer, dancing, or watching *Dr. Quinn, Medicine Woman.* It was a quaint, simple, happy childhood.

But, as the weeks went on, I would come to find out my mom's cancer was advanced.

First, it was inoperable, then it had spread to her lymph nodes, and beyond.

She started chemo and radiation, but had to travel three hours each way to a regional facility for treatment, as no options for treatment were available at that time at our rural healthcare facilities.

She became sick quickly, and you could tell her body was breaking down and fragile. She lost a lot of weight on her already petite frame, and the sparkle in her smile and eyes was dulled.

In June, she was having "a good day" at home, where she had spent the day cooking a meal from scratch. That day ended with her having a stroke in our hallway. I had to call 911 because she was unresponsive. An ambulance came to pick her up as she couldn't talk or move. It was a traumatic experience and the beginning of the end. Within a day, she was transferred by ambulance to the regional facility St. Mary's Medical Center, and within a month, she was moved to hospice. We spent the remainder of the summer in Duluth, essentially waiting for her to die.

The hospice hours were the worst. By then, I had finally started to realize that she wasn't going to make it. How do you make the best of it? When asked what she was going to do in heaven, she would say that she was excited to see her dad and other relatives who had passed. She also told us she wanted to be a "ballerina". This made me smile.

Reality was a foggy state at this point for me. I was told she was going to die, but I didn't really accept or process it. That's the thing about reality in those situations. It's hard to confront it. I certainly didn't have the cognitive skills to know how to navigate what was to come.

The shock hit me, too. Repeatedly, then and for years afterwards. I didn't understand why this was happening to me, to my mom, to my family. Why was something so traumatic happening? We were good people.

That was the lesson. Both amazing and terrible things happen each day to both good and bad people alike.

Innocent people get killed in car accidents, children get murdered in schools, and yet you could win a multi-million-dollar lottery ticket, find the love of your life online, and conceive a child you never thought you'd have in a test tube.

You could also one day learn that your two-year-old child has cancer.

When people say that life is a wild ride, figuratively, yes, absolutely, but that is really just the half of it.

People, most adults anyway, somewhat know that unexpected things happen. You just try not to ever think of the worst. I mean, why would you? I get it. I did it.

The question we will all face at some point is, will you have the mental and emotional skills needed when you are about to take a steep fall on the roller coaster? Will you be able to hang on? Will you be run over? Will you be decapitated? Will you be able to process? Will you accept what has been handed to you? Will you be forever changed? Will you let these things control you and your life path? Will you use them for good? For bad?

Will you be able to see the light—your light—in the darkness? Will you chase it? Will you work to illuminate it?

I believe that this concept is a continuum. It's not a one-and-done where the significant life event has presented, and that's it. You overcome. I may have thought that prior to 2021, but certainly not after! Not now!

You will be required to continually evolve, adapt, change, and accept. I didn't know that at age fifteen, honestly. But how could I have known? I was a child. I also didn't really know that at age thirty-seven, either. I was oblivious in thinking I had already been through the worst life had to offer.

So, my advice: Be prepared for the unexpected. Life is full of it. I didn't like the ride I was forced to be on with my mom or my child.

No choice, though, here I was. Strapping in. I instinctively knew I had to be there for my child. I couldn't think about myself or my emotions in that moment. He needed my strength.

The expression "Your child is a reflection of your heart on the outside of your body" is true. There really is not a beginning or ending. He is me and I am him. He came from me. I'm sure my mom felt this too, and that is one of the reasons she couldn't bear to break my heart by talking much about her impending death.

Coming back from my memories, emotions and the trauma related to my mom's illness, I now found myself in Ollie's hospital room.

I rested my body by lying down and then hopped up each time the night nurses came in to check vitals or for other necessities. I didn't know what I was supposed to do, but I wanted to make myself helpful and knowledgeable about what was going on with Ollie. He was so little and only had select words. I was going to have to be his eyes and ears.

Each time I hopped up, my mind was racing, and I couldn't stop staring at Ollie in his bed. These nurses came in a lot. They really had their work cut out for them! Every hour? At least every two. I had no idea how much monitoring and attentiveness Ollie would need. I had no idea what my new role was in all this.

Too much newness.

Too much uncertainty.

Too much sadness.

I found myself back in a foggy cognitive state. Standing beside Ollie's hospital crib, in my pajamas, with my silicone sandals on, wondering again, is this even real? I didn't have the capacity to accept it yet.

The following morning, I was exhausted, sad, scared, and yet somehow hopeful. It was like those prayers kicked in. It was a wave of more calmness than I had felt in my whole life. Intuitively, as bad as this situation was, I felt we were in the right place to get Ollie the help he needed. I could feel it. I could see it. How amazing that this children's hospital existed ten miles from our home! How astounding that they found the cancer type so quickly, and we could be here and start treatment. A stark comparison to my mom's experience with diagnosis and treatment.

While there was still mostly uncertainty, I did think, for whatever reason, that what we were dealing with was curable. For that, I am so very grateful. I knew that treatments had advanced greatly in twenty years.

We would rapidly have information shared with us over the coming days and months.

While we did keep our faith and hope, we would endure the greatest mental and physical marathon we hope to ever run.

We would find light in the most unexpected places.

We would be lifted like a cloud by our family, friends and community, sometimes people we didn't even know. So many acts of kindness, generosity and love were bestowed upon us. We were on prayer chains and in weekly intercessions.

It will be a journey that I will never forget and that has forever changed me and our family.

The coming pages document the often day-to-day account of Oliver's cancer journey from his most unexpected diagnosis and the start of chemo treatment in October of 2021, all the way through to November of 2023.

With the need and desire to inform family and friends of what was going on, limited personal and emotional capacity to call, text, or email updates, it was suggested that I use an online platform called

CaringBridge. This platform was more private for sharing Ollie's health updates. While in the hospital, we had little access to the outside world. With the pandemic, no visitors were allowed, not even immediate family like siblings or grandparents. Honestly, though, that was probably for the best. The thought of taking visitors through all this seemed very daunting. All my physical, emotional, and mental energy went to caring for my child.

The intent in sharing our story is that you gain perspective into finding ways each day—through the good and bad, happy and sad, anxious and productive—to find a spot to hold on to hope.

To always choose to chase the light, to stand in it, whatever "light" means to you. Let it illuminate you in both big and small ways.

I also chose to share Oliver's story so that one day, when and if he wants, he can read the details of his brave story of survival. By the grace of God, Ollie remembers very little about his actual cancer treatment and the experience I share here in this book.

CHAPTER 5

THE UNKNOWN

As I was considering starting the CaringBridge journal site, it was challenging to know just how to communicate such awful, devastating news. Did I want to? What was the alternative if I didn't? What did I share? What did I not? I knew on some level we were going to be on an extended journey and that we needed to lean into our community for help, but I didn't even know where to start. I wanted to ask for thoughts and prayers. I knew we would need those and that anyone could offer them to us.

My sister Terri asked if she could start a meal train, an online platform to help organize meals and gift cards for meals, and I reluctantly agreed. It, like many things we would be offered and given in the coming days and months, was difficult to accept. Mostly because we didn't know when we would even be home to receive food or other thoughtful gifts. We were at the hospital now for the indefinite future, and once we got out, I didn't know how long we would be able to be home. So much uncertainty. Also, contextually, we had jobs, we had insurance, we had money, a nice home, we had a community of support. We didn't feel worthy of the showering of help and love that was bestowed upon us. It was difficult to acknowledge that, despite all these things being in place, we would need to, and would want to, accept help. No going around it, even if in the moment we were naïve about it.

Please keep in mind as you read the following pages: the Caring-Bridge Chronicles were almost exclusively typed on my phone on the App, reporting out from a hospital room, often lying on a small sofa bed that Brian and I shared, after both Brian and Ollie had fallen asleep at night. The room would be dark except for the glow from the lights from the various machines, IV pumps and my phone. Writing was a tremendous outlet for me during this dark time, both literally and figuratively—a few moments to myself when I could recount and reflect on the day's activities and find something to be thankful for. Writing helped me process, to some extent, what was going on.

Also, as time allowed, I was able to read the extensive feedback given on the posts by what I would come to call "our tribe," which grew and grew and grew to include many people we had never met.

I knew that while I was alone in sharing Ollie's story each day, that once complete, many people were receiving the notification of a new post, and they were with me. So many people cared and shared with us. They were letting us know that they were in it with us, too. That was very comforting.

The extent to who knew what was going on prior to the Caring-Bridge posts was very limited to those who needed to know; Brian's parents, our siblings, our best friends, Ollie's daycare, and our employers. CaringBridge offered us a way to communicate Ollie's story in a way that felt acceptable to us. It was our public-facing narrative of what was going on. It wasn't always pretty, but we did try to stay mostly positive and hopeful. The BEHIND-THE-SCENES thoughts that are included were not shared on the platform and will bring additional context and perspective into our world as it was at the time.

CaringBridge Chronicles

October 29, 2021

It is with much sadness and shock we are sharing some very difficult news about Ollie that has evolved over this past week.

We took Ollie to urgent care Sunday, October 24, to get checked for COVID and a persistent bellyache. He has been saying his belly hurts on and off for a few weeks now, but this past weekend it got worse after he fell on the playground on Friday after school. I was talking with some girlfriends on Sunday afternoon, and they said the Delta variant often presents itself as gastrointestinal in toddlers, so we should investigate his general bellyache for that, if nothing else.

He has had what we would characterize as a "bloated belly" but looked like a toddler belly on and off for months. Nothing seemed abnormal.

On Sunday, October 24, at urgent care, they took all his vitals, a COVID test, and an x-ray of his belly.

Negative on virus and blood oxygen normal.

The Nurse Practitioner said that it looked like he was really gassy/constipated. They gave him an enema and some MiraLAX and sent us home. Monday, October 25, in the morning, they called us back and said the radiologist wanted us back in immediately, but this time to the ER at Cardinal Glennon Children's Hospital in St. Louis.

Monday, October 25, was an absolute nightmare of a day, and we are honestly still processing. Essentially, a CT scan and subsequent blood work revealed a large mass in Ollie's abdomen that was cancerous. They admitted him that evening to the oncology ward. We have been with him this whole time. Monday evening, he was set up for a blood transfusion as his red blood cell count was low. He was able to get that successfully overnight while sleeping and being closely monitored. An MRI was ordered for Tuesday to get further imaging of his mass and spine and pelvis area.

Ollie had his MRI Tuesday, October 26, and they were able to get a much clearer picture of where they think the tumor is coming from, his liver, and their thought on what type of cancer it was. They also checked his spinal cord, which was normal. No other masses were revealed in the imaging.

The surgeon came and spoke with us that evening about evaluating if the tumor could be removed. His plan was to remove the tumor and part of his liver Wednesday (October 27) if it could be safely resected. The problem they expressed was the tumor's proximity to the portal vein.

If they couldn't take it out, they would perform a biopsy, and he would then likely start chemo as soon as possible (ASAP) to shrink the tumor and then take it out. This kind of tumor must come out.

Further blood tests confirmed cancer type.

Hepatoblastoma.

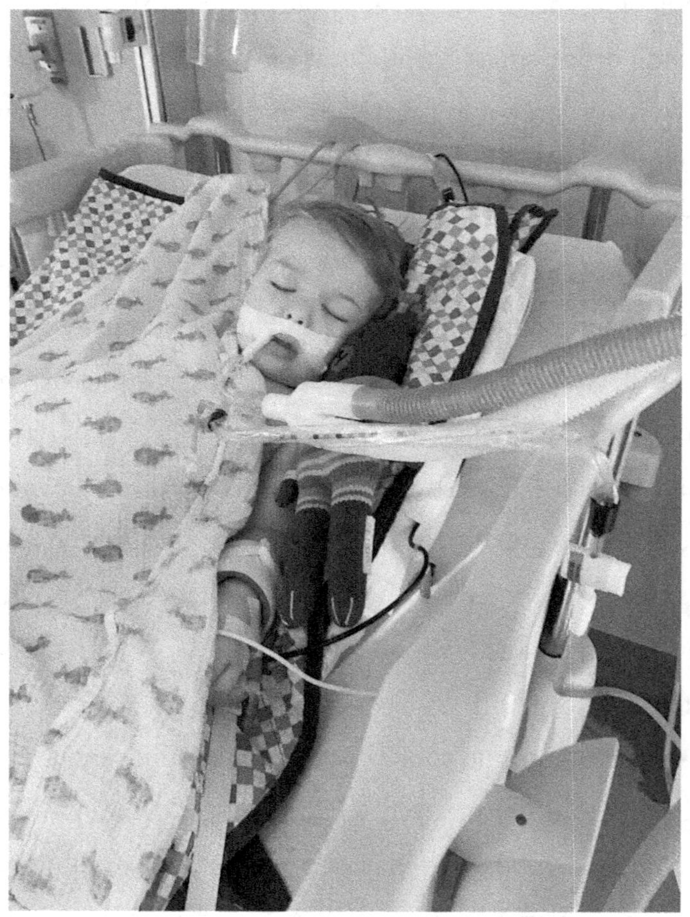

Surgery revealed that at this time, the tumor could not be removed. It is too close to portal vein. It is also very vascular in composition, and because of that, Ollie lost a lot of blood in surgery. He had to have several transfusions. After three plus hours, they had the biopsy completed and put in his central port for treatment.

He was sedated and intubated for the surgery and overnight, and into the next day. He went immediately to the Pediatric Intensive Care Unit (PICU) that evening to be closely monitored. Brian and I were so thankful that we could stay in his PICU room with him. The surgeon visited us and gave us an update of the surgery and his thoughts in general about what he saw. Despite the tumor not being able to be removed, it had not wrapped itself around the portal vein. He also thought that with treatment, hopefully the tumor would shrink, and we could get it out, eventually.

It was one of the most difficult nights of our lives to hear this information and see our baby like that. Thursday, October 28, late morning, they were able to take him off the sedation and ventilation in PICU and wake him up. It was such a relief to have him back, talking, looking at us. He immediately asked for a sucker and Mickey Mouse Clubhouse, which made us smile. He was able to get out of the PICU on Thursday evening, and we were moved back to a room in the oncology ward.

He is doing as good as could be expected with close monitoring of his many different pain medications, and we were able to hold our boy. It was a long night for him, trying to get comfortable. But our care team is amazing.

Friday, October 29, we were presented with his treatment options. The surgeon and his oncologist are hoping to start his chemo on Monday, November 1, if we can.

He just completed another blood transfusion today; are hoping that his red blood cell count will improve and he can continue to recover from surgery this weekend.

It has been a long, traumatic week to say the least for all of us, but especially our Ollie. We have had so much information coming at us quickly. He has had so many tests, procedures, major surgery. We feel so fortunate to be working with world-class doctors who seem to think he will be able to be cured. But we know we have a long road of treatment and surgery ahead of us. We need as many prayers and positive thoughts as you can send, and appreciate each person who has reached out to express concern and love. We will try to keep this page updated as our primary form of communication moving forward.

BEHIND-THE-SCENES

As I sat on the sofa in Ollie's hospital room writing the very first CaringBridge post on my phone, I thought to myself, *How do you even go about communicating something like this?* I knew I had to be delicate. With Ollie being so young, I was in charge of his privacy. But to me, sharing the details of his situation mattered. He was in a serious and precarious condition, and we needed prayers. The shock and devotion poured out of me, wanting people to know and understand what Ollie, Brian and I were up against.

As I quickly learned more about the different medical tests and terms, I tried to share. It was a significant learning process for me.

I have never had an MRI, CT scan, or many of the tests Ollie has had, such as an electrocardiogram (EKG) or echocardiogram (ECHO). I have never received a blood transfusion. I have never had cancer.

I had no idea how many people would follow Ollie's story so intently, offering words of encouragement in comments with each post. It felt like I was reporting from the front lines— "the lines" being the children's oncology ward. For us and many others, it was a war of sorts.

A war on cancer. It was a very difficult environment to be in. All the kids on this floor, from babies to teens, had cancer. All the parents were in the boat in various stages of the storm with you.

All these kids were fighting for their lives. It wasn't something that you can adequately describe if you haven't lived it, but I was going to try my hardest to give an essence of what we saw, felt and heard as Ollie went through this. In terms of the type of cancer Ollie was diagnosed with, hepatoblastoma, approximately 4,000 children worldwide are diagnosed annually. That equates to one to two cases per million kids globally.

October 31, 2021

Ollie has been resting this weekend. The hospital is very quiet on the weekend, which has been welcomed by us all.

His spirits have been as good as can be expected considering everything he has and continues to experience. He is talking, smiling, asking questions, being his normal sweet self.

On Friday, the staff brought a fun bag to each child's door and dressed up for Halloween and did a parade through the halls, bringing goodies; no candy, but fun things like crayons, stickers, and little stuffed toys/trinkets; stuff kids love to hold in their hands and play with. I have all of it in a bag and am giving Ollie one or two each day as his "surprises." He really thinks that is fun.

He deserves little bits of fun wherever we can create them. He is off the narcotic pain killers, and his care team has been diligently watching his pain and managing it well.

It's still a lot of medicine, but we all feel like he is making baby steps in the right direction.

His hemoglobin levels have also remained constant since his transfusion on Friday afternoon. He even requested spicy taco meat today for lunch.

He loves his tacos at Lakeside Children's Academy, and I got the sense that tacos reminded him of something familiar. He was very happy to sit and eat.

Tomorrow (November 1), our goal is to start day one of Round-1 of chemo treatment. He is expected to have two rounds and then his next scan. If the scan reveals the tumor has shrunk, then surgery will be scheduled near the end of December or early January.

He will need additional rounds of chemo following his surgery. If the tumor does not shrink after two rounds, he will continue treatment until it does. We are praying this phase can begin tomorrow, that it successfully treats this tumor, and that the side effects, both short and long term, are not too difficult or scary for him. Keep praying for us all, we feel it and need it. We are truly working to take each day at a time.

BEHIND-THE-SCENES

I was blown away at our experiences with the Child Life Services at Cardinal Glennon Children's Hospital. This included the staff who provided these specific resources, but also, as I discuss throughout the experience, the nurses and doctors who just thought of the kids as kids and tried their best to treat them that way. The Halloween parade was so cute, thoughtful, and something for these kids to celebrate and feel like they, too, got to have a Halloween holiday.

For me, the human parade was both a happy and sad experience. A juxtaposition of sorts. We had a Mickey Mouse costume for Ollie at home, and of course, it wasn't one of the items we grabbed when packing a bag for the hospital when we got the emergency call a few days earlier.

Not that he would have worn it there anyway. But the thought of missing Halloween was strange and sad. All of Ollie's classmates in daycare would be having a Halloween parade of their own at his school, and here we were in the hospital oncology ward. It was a surreal experience and a prime example of appreciating the light in the darkness from wherever you are, in that moment in time.

November 1, 2021

NO CHEMO TODAY.

Despite what feels like a small setback, we know that our care team is doing their very best to evaluate Ollie's condition for tolerating the intense chemo. This includes looking at a variety of vitals for consistency.

His hemoglobin dropped by a point from yesterday to today, and his team of doctors felt it was best to wait until tomorrow to reevaluate this metric to ensure it doesn't continue to drop. Because he is so little and just had such a major surgery five days ago, where he lost over 300cc of blood, their approach is extra cautious. If the hemoglobin does continue to drop tomorrow, he will likely need another blood transfusion before he can start his chemo.

This could delay us further.

The waiting game is hard. But this precious time with our boy feels special. He had a good day. First thing this a.m., he wanted to color and play; we went on many walks with his new Mickey Mouse backpack, including all the way to the atrium and other areas of Cardinal Glennon to check out these unique clocks they have in various locations and hallways.

On one trip down to the lower level, while waiting for the elevator, we ran into the volunteer with the library cart and got a new book, which he loved. He requested pasta for lunch. He was really acting and sounding like his sweet, funny self today. That made us feel so happy for him.

So many people have continuously reached out, offering help in any way, dropped off care packages at our home and hospital; sent cards, gift cards, gifts in the mail. We are blown away and without words for your generosity and kindness. We feel so supported by our circle of love and this institution. Praying for a night of rest and the ability to start his treatment tomorrow. Keep the prayers coming. Each hour is unquestionably unique and hard.

But we promise you all that we, as a family, are staying strong and positive despite the obstacles ahead of us.

BEHIND-THE-SCENES

The walks we would go on, even with "tubie" as we would come to call his IV pole, were so incredibly therapeutic. The weekends were always very quiet at the hospital, and we could really go explore without encountering a lot of people in the hallways. This also helped us kill time and get some movement in while learning the lay of the land at Cardinal Glennon. Our favorite surprises were always the random grandfather clocks, each with its own theme, and beautiful artwork adorning the walls that had been donated over the years.

Sometimes on these walks, we would run into the volunteer who ran the book cart or who handled Thor, the therapy dog. It was always extra special to have a minute to pick out a new book to bring back to our room or to pet the dog.

These walks were also not without anxiety, though. Imagine a two-year-old navigating walking with a movable pole that has an IV line connected to him? We had to move with "tubie" very carefully and intently.

I frequently had a visual nightmare of Ollie falling or deciding to run, and the IV line getting ripped out of his chest port. Thankfully, that never happened.

CHAPTER 6

FIRST ROUND

November 2, 2021

ROUND-1 DAY 1

Finally, after waiting all day for his metrics to be correct to safely administer the chemo infusions of Cisplatin, his first bag has been hung. These metrics included hemoglobin and hydration levels. Each time he gets chemo treatments, these metrics must be met. It's a purposeful process.

It's overwhelming yet amazing to think that only seven days ago, we found out what type of cancer Ollie faced, and today we start day 1 of treatment.

Cardinal Glennon's team has been swiftly and methodically working to get us to this day of hope. This main chemo infusion will be administered over six hours, followed by two others and by two protectant type drugs.

For the Cisplatin, the main side effects can be some hearing loss and heart issues.

We pray that the chemicals work to reduce the tumor and that our baby is spared any major side effects of these drugs that are required to be administered to save his life.

Our cousin Betsy sent us some incredibly special sacramental items to offer comfort, hope, and protection. I blessed Ollie with them as they started his first chemo treatment today. This included Lourdes Holy Water, St. Jude Oil, Medals of St. Jude, and the Miraculous Medal, which I have tied to his crib. We are also praying on Ollie's Great-Grandma Geen's rosary, asking for an intercession.

My dear friend Lauren gifted me a St. Peregrine medallion that I have been wearing. I have also been praying to my mother, Ollie's Grandma Colleen, as well as his Great-Grandma Sagitto, who both lost their lives to cancer. I know we have many special angels watching over our entire family.

I just took a deep breath as I think about tonight and tomorrow and hope.

Hope that this treatment works. Hope that Ollie is as comfortable as can be. Hope that the treatments don't make him too sick. Hope that we can eventually go home in the next few days until he starts another round of treatment next week.

Thank you for your continued thoughts, prayers, messages of strength, and support.

BEHIND-THE-SCENES

What I didn't feel comfortable sharing at the time was how I felt the moment the medical professionals walked in with their full hazmat suits on, as required when administering the chemo.

It was startling to see this, to say the least. I, immediately alarmed, thought, "You are in a hazmat suit to protect yourself from these drugs, the same drugs that will be put directly into the veins of my child."

I wasn't mad at the nurses, but mad at the situation and just so scared. While I knew we had a choice not to treat, which in Ollie's case would have resulted in death, the alternative, chemo treatment, was heartbreaking. It wasn't one chemo either, but five toxic chemo drugs my child would have injected into his body for months. It's heartbreaking to see an adult go through cancer treatment, and that's magnified for a young child who has no idea what is happening to them.

While I felt like we had a good plan for treatment, I was also so scared for Ollie with the potential side effects we were warned of, partial or full hearing loss and/or heart damage. Potential infertility, something I didn't share online. Again, the ability to be able to have your child live, in remission, as a result of taking these drugs—even if they must suffer the side effects—is truly amazing, but the situation seems so incredibly unfair.

Anyone going through complex medical issues is faced with many decisions daily that leave little room for options for desired outcomes. I felt like all I could do was pray that Ollie would be spared at least some of the nasty side effects and that the cancer would respond to the treatment. Mostly, I was just so thankful that we had choices.

November 3, 2021

Tonight marks our tenth night at Cardinal Glennon, and we are hoping and praying that we get to go home tomorrow.

I would have never imagined we would be here this long. So far, the side effects from the first chemo, Cisplatin, have been minimal today.

This is in part due to many preventive nausea drugs that are staged. Thank God.

We were happy that Ollie wanted to get up and go for a walk on our floor. He also requested his "instruments," and the musical therapist came by to show him a variety of instruments he could play.

He picked the tambourine. His teachers and friends at Lakeside Children's Academy probably are not surprised by this. He loves playing instruments.

We were also able to get him to wear a mask outside his room for the first time, which is so very important due to his immunocompromised condition now.

To entice him to do this, a Child Life specialist arranged for us to get some solo play for him in a special playroom for toddlers. He was happy and kept telling her, "Thank you."

I cannot say enough how amazing the staff here is. Little wins each day will help us stay positive and strong for our boy. Two different chemo infusions tonight around midnight.

We thank each one of you for your continued prayers of healing, strength, and protection.

November 4, 2021

Home. Sweet. Home.

These words take on a whole different meaning after the events of the past ten days. Life is so fragile and precious.

Yes, we all know this figuratively, but to experience it literally puts things into such perspective.

To think of all the things that had to go right for us to be home right now is amazing.

Thank you for all your prayers. We feel them. They are working. Keep them coming. We know that thank you doesn't begin to cover it, but for the many doctors, nurses, resource specialists, our family and friends who have helped us carry some of this load during this time, we are forever grateful.

As we were walking out into the fresh air, Ollie requested to go to the park before even going home. While we couldn't make that request happen today, Brian and I had to smile because it demonstrated to us that his sweet soul has not been deterred by this awful situation.

He also has tolerated the treatments just fine so far.

We are hoping for five uneventful days of recovery, for him and for us, until his next chemo infusion scheduled for Tuesday (November 9). This treatment is planned as outpatient at the Costas Center at Cardinal Glennon. He will then follow that treatment with the same outpatient chemo treatment seven days later to end his Round-1 of treatment.

One day at a time, we will make it through.

The family across the hall was with their four-year-old son Beckett, who was diagnosed with B Cell ALL Leukemia a week before Ollie was diagnosed with Hepatoblastoma. Before we left today, they gave me a bracelet that says, "Faith over Fear." And I couldn't have said it better myself.

We all can't wait to sleep in our own beds tonight.

BEHIND-THE-SCENES

When you return home to a place that looks the same as you left it, but your life is now completely different, it is a foreign experience. To me, it felt very surreal, strange and sad.

I longed to be the same human I was before I left my home for Cardinal Glennon ten days prior, when my worries were much lighter. When my life was what it was then. Your home, your safe space, along with your personal being, is now a ground zero of sorts. A shell of what it was. Yes, the things are all still there, the memories are all still there, but physically being in the space as it was felt like a painful reminder of "what was." But the reality was that everything had changed. In a blink. From here on out, nothing was the same, and nothing would ever be the same. My child had cancer. Our recalibration of life was just beginning. I knew I would emerge from this experience much different than I was before, whether I liked it or not. I had to be mindful of that.

But I was also physically weak. Weak from the intense stress and pain that my body, mind and soul had endured the past ten days.

Weak from not eating or sleeping properly due to the stress and pain, and the nature of living at a hospital.

In those first ten days, I didn't leave the hospital once to even go outside. I should have, but I didn't. I did explore inside the hospital walls as described on our walks with "tubie," but didn't interact with many people outside our medical team except through CaringBridge. I was brave one day and went to the hospital lobby to meet a friend who wanted to give me a hug and a meal she had cooked. I say brave because I didn't want to see anyone. That made the situation feel more real. That felt more difficult. I felt like I wasn't strong enough just yet. I could hide in the hospital room for the time being. And that is what I did until we left that first time.

On the day we left, feeling the fresh air in my lungs and on my skin was a renewal of sorts. It felt like a bath for my soul. It also snapped me out of a daze that I needed to shake. I would have to work hard to take care of myself during these hospital stays. How to do this was yet to be determined, but I would need to muster the strength I never knew I had to mentally get us all through it. I would need to do it differently than I had done in those first few days

Upon our return home, we had a lot of life strategizing and continued recalibration to do. We now needed to keep our home as clean as possible. I remember deep cleaning my kitchen and fridge first. It was therapeutic to some degree. I wanted to make sure that the food and medicines that needed cold storage were in a clean environment. We also needed to rearrange some aspects of our home to make it more comfortable for both Ollie and us. This included converting our living room into more of a playroom. Getting some new cozy essentials, such as blankets and space rugs. Also, putting together a couple of small baskets that would be easily moveable with hand sanitizer, diapers, ointment, lip balm, and other medical essentials.

Getting a handle on Ollie's various medications, there were so many, was overwhelming to say the least. First, having them filled at the local pharmacy. Then, figuring out the timing for administration based on what was provided to us and what he needed was the next obstacle. Timing was of the essence, and we were actively, in real-time, learning what Ollie needed and tolerated. What was optional for him and what was not.

We quickly learned that the anti-nausea and anti-anxiety medications were key factors in helping him feel better. We had a binder with the information and also started a separate notebook where we tracked all his medications, food intake and bowel movements. With so much to manage, we really knew we needed to stay organized and be able to have a reference if asked by his care team about anything specific.

Also, we needed to find help in caring for Ollie when he was home, so Brian and I could each work at least part-time. Work was a whole separate topic, and we both were going to need to navigate what work looked like now, especially me, as I carried our health insurance. Luckily, I worked from home and could continue to work remotely at the hospital when I could, in between doctor visits, at night once Ollie was asleep, and any open time that appeared. Taking an extended leave of absence or quitting my job at this time was altogether not an option. Brian and I had the difficult conversation on day two in the hospital that if one of us needed to step away from our job, it would have to be him.

I felt tremendous mom guilt about this, but it was what it was.

While I can attest to saying our employers were kind and reasonable with us, navigating filing job protection granted under the Family and Medical Leave Act (FMLA), while working through the grief and overwhelm of the general situation, in a hospital room, was extremely challenging. So was focusing on work. Brian and I both worked in demanding business development roles, so our jobs depended on interacting with clients. Did we tell our customers what we were going through? Should we?

At first, I chose not to. I couldn't yet have a conversation about the situation without crying.

I wasn't prepared to answer questions. I also worried that people might choose to not do business with me if they knew my attention was not 100% at work. Or they might not like that I might be out on leave for an extended period. In hindsight, this sounds silly, but in the moment, we needed to keep our jobs to make money to pay our bills, like our mortgage, and I especially needed to keep our health insurance.

Also, the constant check-ins from the insurance case manager assigned to Ollie's case were very challenging for me. I'll call her Ann for short.

Ann started calling me and leaving messages on my voicemail before we even left the hospital the first time, probing for as much information as I would give her about Ollie's condition, which I decided would be limited. I knew she was assigned to his case to evaluate his case risk profile. Throughout Ollie's journey, Ann would check in with me at least once a week. She was never a source of comfort but rather one of agitation.

November 8, 2021

Long before this current situation we are in, and to this day, one of my favorite bible verses is "I hereby command you: Be strong and courageous; do not be frightened or dismayed, for the Lord your God is with you wherever you go." (Joshua 1:9, NRSV-CE). Reflecting on these words characterizes how Ollie has been handling his "bellyache."

Strong and courageous.

Hanging in there.

Rolling with it.

Trying, despite not feeling great and clearly knowing things are different, and not getting too discouraged.

Exactly two weeks ago today, we heard that terrifying word, CANCER.

What? How? Why?

We were faced with complete devastation and disbelief. But in that moment and throughout this nightmare, we also knew that we had to try to hold it together at least in front of Ollie so that he could see we were being strong too.

The last few days, it has felt so good to be home and in our own space, reestablishing our "new normal."

Getting a hold on all the medicines has still been overwhelming. Ollie has done tremendously well considering everything. We have been able to get him to rest, to eat, to walk, to ride his bike, to go to a park. We even stopped by the Kirkwood Public Library for a book.

He was able to see his Grandma and Grandpa Geen. While our visits have been shorter as he is more tired, he has been an absolute trooper wearing a mask in public.

Brian and I were so grateful to get our COVID boosters on Saturday. A huge win to helping protect our family.

We have also been able to focus on him exclusively thanks to the outpouring of love and generosity from all of you in meals and gift cards. It helps make our time at home easier.

Tomorrow is our outpatient day at Cardinal Glennon Costas Center for his next dose of chemo.

We are hoping it goes smoothly and that his lab tests don't indicate that he will also need a blood and/or platelet transfusion.

We are also hoping for continued minimal side effects–with the help of powerful anti-nausea meds. We are hoping and praying for continued strength, courage, and patience from us all. As you can see, we have a lot of hope.

We appreciate your prayers, thoughts, and good vibes. If you can give blood or platelets, please consider. If you've never done it before, it's very easy and relatively painless.

November 9, 2021

Quick post to update on our outpatient visit at Costas Center today. Chemo infusion went smoothly, and our clinic visit was quick. We were in and out in three hours. Most importantly, no transfusions needed as lab results looked good. We will wait on alpha-fetoprotein (AFP) numbers for a day or so. This will tell us a little about how the tumor could be responding. Ollie did amazing.

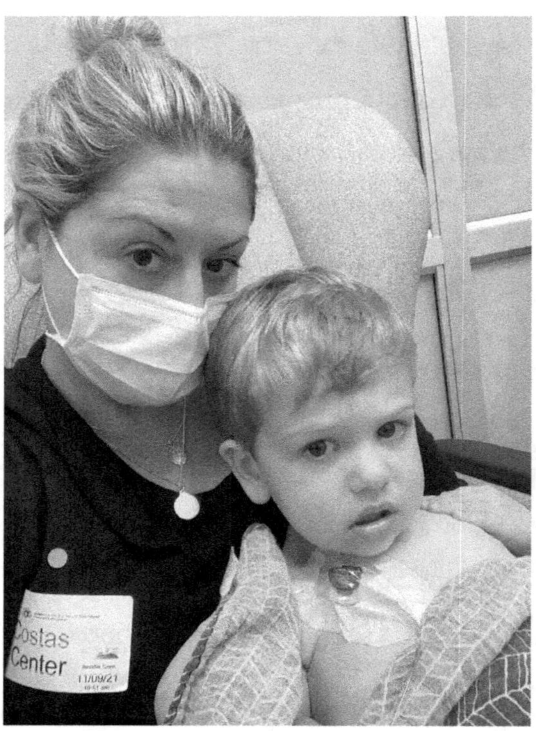

When he was done with his treatment, he was surprised to find out he got to pick a toy from the toy closet. This is all thanks to the Friends of Kids with Cancer organization. Nice little touches all around to help these kids cope. Keep the prayers coming. Same chemo infusion next Tuesday.

November 12, 2021

Friday update: I know when life gives you lemons, you need to make "lemonade."

We made the lemonade, but this version tastes sour.

What to do? Add sweetness? We just didn't have it in us this week.

Thank God for others. Truly. I don't even know what to say other than we are completely blown away. Speechless.

Tears of overwhelm in disbelief.

So, to each one of you—our family, our friends, our neighbors, and our colleagues who have helped us with an outpouring of sweet, thoughtful, pure kindness—thank you.

So many prayers, messages, meals, gift cards, gifts. We can't express our gratitude enough. You are helping lift us up.

This week, in addition to Ollie's treatment and constant care, we have tried to transition to finding our "new normal."

It has been admittedly exhausting and challenging. But we will get it figured out, eventually. And the general slowdown in life isn't terrible.

The good news is Ollie has been doing great, considering everything. Minimal side effects from his chemo on Tuesday; less energy, irritability, some loss of appetite, but still eating sporadically. No nausea or vomiting.

We have been told to expect hair loss soon, so we are anticipating that. But we have been able to get out to the playground and the market and do some things that make Ollie, Brian and me feel like life isn't completely different now.

One day at a time!

November 16, 2021

DAY 15

Final day in the first treatment cycle.

We made it. Round-1 done.

Thank you, God. Thank you, science.

Ollie did great again, despite obviously knowing that where we were, Cardinal Glennon, is not a fun place for him. He got upset for his vitals: height, weight, temperature, blood pressure, and blood oxygen.

Thankfully, for his port access, we were prescribed lidocaine numbing cream to put on it before we leave the house, so it shouldn't hurt for him. He doesn't flinch when it's inserted. The port is such a vital tool, as that is how they administer his chemo medications, but also draw blood for his weekly labs. He is such a strong boy when they access the port and draw blood and hook up his IVs.

His blood count labs were lower this week. This is to be somewhat expected as we go along. Especially his white blood, hemoglobin, and overall CBC counts.

He did not need a transfusion today, but this could impact if we are able to start day 1 of Round-2 next Monday, where he will be admitted again. If we are not able to, treatment will be delayed a week or so.

We must be extra careful for the next few days.

He is at high risk for getting sick as his immune system is very compromised. We also must watch for signs that he may need a transfusion.

His doctor came and talked with us at length about next steps. First is Round-2 of chemo. Then that third week of the second round, he will get another set of scans, CT and MRI to see how the tumor is looking.

Then the plan will be to continue chemo, or surgery, then more chemo.

Either way, the tumor must come out.

I mentioned AFP in my last post. AFP is a cancer marker for Hepatoblastoma. We did find out Friday that the AFP test from last week increased by about 600 from the original test that was completed October 25.

The doctor said this wasn't ideal, but no immediate cause for concern, as the jump, in the scheme of things, was relatively low and hadn't been measured in a few weeks. It will be important when the AFP is measured again at the next treatment that it is lower.

The situation is very fluid. We are doing our best to take everything as it comes, one day at a time, while also not looking too far out. Keep the prayers coming.

BEHIND-THE-SCENES

The lingering pandemic at this time caused an extended layer of strain on many, but especially those who were considered immunocompromised, like Ollie.

Things in life had not yet returned to "normal" or a "pre-pandemic" state for most people. Many workplaces had not resumed in-office activities, or if they had, done so in a limited context, such as implementing hybrid work schedules.

Some schools were remote or hybrid, with masks required when in session. A vaccine and boosters had been approved for adults, but not yet for children. While in general, the pandemic virus wasn't as life-threatening as initially thought, it had proven to be unpredictable and inconsistent, with different symptoms and outcomes appearing for individuals.

In fact, most people knew someone who had died of COVID. For me, it was my longtime hairstylist Erin; her father died of the virus in the early onset of the pandemic. No underlying conditions, his body just couldn't overcome it. Brian had more than one client die of it. It was very scary.

The combined factors of the pandemic and cancer made our experience in living through cancer much more isolating. We tried our hardest to not put Ollie or ourselves in situations where we knew people who would not be vaccinated would be present, but that was a tall order. That pretty much meant very limited exposure to the public.

Anytime we chose to interact with people in a close environment, we were potentially putting ourselves or Ollie at risk. So, we did all we could do. We always wore masks in public, including Ollie. We carried hand sanitizer with us and in our vehicles, something we still do. We practiced the best hygiene and hand washing we could. We stayed in hibernation mode most of the time.

While COVID wasn't the only virus we were worried about Ollie contracting, it felt like the scariest because there were so many unknowns about it and it seemed to keep evolving into different variants.

November 18, 2021

Four North (4N)–Again.

Well, Ollie unfortunately spiked a high fever after his nap yesterday. Cheeks were flushed when he woke up, and his little hands and feet were hot. I took his temp, and it was consistently reading 102-103.

We are required to call Cardinal Glennon immediately for any fever over 101.4, as fevers are a major cause for concern for infection in the bloodstream for cancer patients.

The on-call doctor told us to bring him in right away and pack a bag, as we would likely be staying at least a day or two.

Of course, we were less than thrilled to tell him we had to go back to the hospital. Poor boy has been through so much in four short weeks. And we have only been home for two.

They got us in right away at the ER and took his blood samples. They told us he would be admitted back to the oncology floor, 4N.

Initial blood labs came back consistent with Tuesday outpatient clinic labs for his chemo treatment, and in some categories, like his neutrophil, white blood cell count increased, all positive.

X-ray came to take a chest photo to scan for pneumonia–that was negative. The COVID swab was negative. They started him on IV antibiotics.

This morning, they told us he tested positive for three common viruses related to common cold/flu. They are now waiting for other cultures to see if anything grows, indicating any additional infection. He is in decent spirits.

He is, of course, confused why he is back in the hospital, and as a result, he is generally anxious and irritated. That is fair.

Fever has been down since last night. It would not be uncommon for it to spike again, so they are watching it closely. He did eat a little breakfast, a blueberry muffin, and is asking to go on a walk, which he can do on our floor with a mask.

He, in general, seems to lack energy today, which is also to be expected, especially after the chemo. Brian and I are adapting as best we can. That is all we can do.

It's a lot, and there is no structure or certainty. For anyone who knows me, I love structure, so I am struggling with that. But we are supporting and loving each other and Ollie as completely as we can while trying to balance work and take care of ourselves.

We are thankful for all the prayers, love, and support from all of you.

We are grateful for our employers, clients, and colleagues who have been understanding and flexible with us.

I am confident that once this nightmare is over, we can do anything.

November 19, 2021

Still here.

Re-admit night three.

Thirteen of the past twenty-six nights we have spent at Cardinal Glennon.

It was an okay day. Started early at 3:45 a.m. because the sense of time is non-existent here. Ollie had a long, late afternoon nap yesterday, and we absolutely wanted him to rest, so we knew it would be an early one this morning.

Lots of coloring, reading, *Mickey Mouse Clubhouse*, and Daniel Tiger today.

We did walk around the floor a few times, and getting out of our room felt great. We have had all the same nurses we had before: Maddy, Kristen, Sarah and Haley. All amazing and sweet.

He had a red blood cell transfusion this afternoon. This is at least transfusion number four for him since we started on this journey.

We feel so fortunate to be in a place where finding blood for his type (O+) and his needs is not an issue, but I do beg all of you: give blood and/or platelets.

The need is so real, and being on the other side of this provides such a different perspective.

Admittedly, I hadn't given blood until December 2019 when my colleague Fran organized a blood drive at work and was recruiting donors. When she approached me about the drive, my answer was the same as it always was, "No. I don't like needles." She told me very frankly, "It's easy and you had a baby, if you can do that, you can certainly give blood." It was easy and painless. I make sure to hydrate well, and now I am one donation away from a gallon of blood. The Red Cross tracks your amount and lets you know where your blood goes.

So, to Francine, "Thank you," and to anyone who hasn't given, just give it a try. I will be signing up to give platelets for the first time in the coming month as well.

Hoping to go home tomorrow. It's looking good. We are scheduled to check back in on Monday for inpatient treatment for a few days.

His labs have improved, and his cultures didn't grow any bacterial infections. He is laughing, talking, and wanting to go home today.

Prayers that we stay fever-free, and all get decent sleep tonight.

BEHIND-THE-SCENES

Watching a family member need blood to live is an eye-opening experience. I had no idea how much blood Ollie would need throughout this cancer journey. It has made me think about trying to amplify our experience to help others. Since I personally never needed a blood transfusion, this need wasn't ever really on my mind. It's truly like a lot of aspects of this medical journey we have been on with our son–hard to have perspective if you haven't personally lived it.

But I'm here to tell you, cancer, blood transfusions, complex and non-complex medical situations are going to come up in your life, for you or a loved one.

Looking for ways to support community institutions is the least we can all do to directly help others who have great needs. Blood is something that is needed universally. We all need it to live. The ask that I amplified during Ollie's treatment was thoughts, prayers, love, and to give blood. What I would come to learn, though, was that the ask for blood is a hard one. Some people can't give blood due to health reasons, some won't give blood because they are terrified of needles and/or blood, and some just don't care or don't want to think about it because it doesn't affect them.

When Ollie had his emergency biopsy surgery on October 27, 2021, to confirm the type of cancer he had, I wrote in the CaringBridge post that he lost a lot of blood during the procedure. We were told that the tumor was vascular in composition and more complex than expected. The details surrounding that day, though, were something I just recently was able to bring myself to review in his notes on MyChart Online. At the time when Ollie was diagnosed, everything happened so fast that I decided that I didn't want to have to interface with the online platform as my source of information.

I wanted to hear it first from the doctors.

No need to worry myself further in finding out information I had no idea how to process. Or, by Googling terms I didn't likely know.

So, I never registered for it until he was through his treatments. The amount of "reminder" texts I would get to sign up for this platform was unreal. Medical systems really want you to use the online option for everything.

Despite that, I just wasn't going to do it. No good could come from anguishing over details in the storm. But I had always wondered about the amount of blood that Ollie lost that day and what it meant.

We knew he was intubated during and after surgery and wound up in the PICU for recovery. That was unexpected, certainly.

In reviewing the notes, I learned that the doctor characterized his tumor with words such as "massive" and "giant," and he lost an estimated 300+ cc of blood during surgery. He received 350 cc to stabilize him. For a two-year-old child, this is considered "significant blood loss", as characterized and described in the Dr.'s notes. And that is why he was left intubated, to reduce the risk of complications from that blood loss.

I'm just so grateful that blood was available to Ollie so that he could be given a chance to live.

November 20, 2021

Home! We were finally discharged this morning and are now home!

Thank you all for your continued support and prayers. We are going to soak up every minute before going back on

CHAPTER 7

SECOND ROUND

Monday, November 22, 2021

DAY 22 ROUND-2, DAY 1.

We made it.

It's like making it to a mile marker in a long-running race. It's an exhale.

Another big win with Ollie meeting his blood and hydration metrics so that he can start Round-2 of treatment today. He should start in about one hour with his Cisplatin. We are so happy to not have any delays. The alternative would have been to wait a week.

Starting again today sets us up for his next outpatient treatment next Tuesday, November 30, and then on December 6, the following week, another outpatient treatment and his first set of CT and MRI scans, since diagnosis.

He is in great spirits and has been doing all sorts of activities. I was finally able to thoughtfully pack before coming today.

He has many options of things to do to help keep himself busy, as we have had so many awesome gifts, projects, books, and art supplies to pick from, thanks to all of you.

Brian and I also used one of our food delivery gift cards to treat ourselves to lunch delivered from Amighetti's, a local Italian sandwich shop. It was delicious. We are so thankful for the generosity and ease in food options during this time.

It will be a long couple of days and nights at Cardinal Glennon, but we are hanging in and hanging on. We are hoping to be discharged Wednesday–Thursday at the latest. We keep hoping, praying, and looking for the light!

BEHIND-THE-SCENES

At this point, we were less than a month into the nightmare. But I did feel like an expert in knowing what we needed to pack for each of us to be as comfortable as we could be for our extended hospital time. This made a big difference in how we could show up for Ollie and how comfortable he felt in the space.

For him, it would be loading up his new Mickey Mouse Backpack and matching cup (thanks, Megan) with all the things to help keep him entertained while being mostly immobile, as well as some of his favorite snacks.

We received many mixed media options for art creation, puzzles, games, figures, and more. We were so grateful to have a rotation of choices to keep play at the forefront of the hospital experience.

For comfort. we brought his little child pillow, OGG quilted blanket, stuffies that he handpicked, always Ollie Bear and Mickey, and his Hatch sound machine.

When we would get to our room, I would try to make the space welcoming and familiar as possible for him.

For Brian and I, we would bring a foam mat to place atop our pull-out futon, pillows, a top sheet, a blanket that was ours and not just one of the hospital's, and a sound machine. I would bring some small comfort items like lavender balm, a sleep mask, hand lotion, Chapstick, and silicone sandals. With those essentials, I established a little ritual for my evening wind-down. Even if I had to be in the hospital, I could do small things for myself to be more comfortable. I would learn that while Ollie napped, I needed to take 30-minute walk breaks, outside if at all possible, so I could get out and breathe the fresh air. I also found that writing in the CaringBridge Journal at night was therapeutic.

November 23, 2021

AFP Decline

Quick update, Ollie has finished all four chemo's and is resting.

Tomorrow we will get a special medicine designed to help his white blood cell count (AFP) recover quicker after these treatments. This must be administered twenty-four hours after his last chemo transfusion, which is 6 p.m. tomorrow. After receiving this and observation for an hour or so, we "should" be able to be discharged.

We are so thankful for our care team for working so hard to try to get us home for the holiday. They are amazing.

Also, we are beyond grateful to share that we received the most positive news on Ollie's AFP levels dropping significantly from the last blood scan two weeks ago.

It is an incredible relief to have some indication that his cancer is responding to the prescribed treatment.

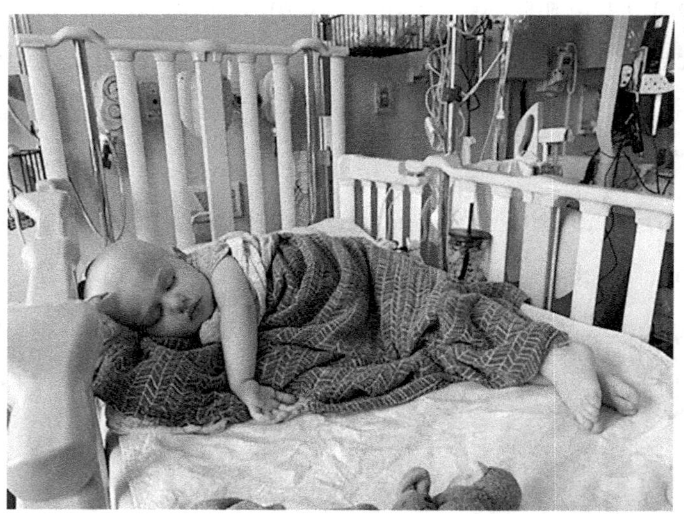

This message today came at a pivotal time, as Brian and I had to make the difficult decision to have Ollie's head shaved, as his hair has been really starting to come out in chunks.

While we certainly know that hair grows back, it is, as my good friend said, the symbolism of it all. Before, you almost wouldn't have known this kid was sick. Now, you know he is a cancer patient. That he is, in fact, really sick.

He was and continues to be brave beyond measure and understanding, as much as a toddler can be.

Thank you for your continued prayers for us three.

BEHIND-THE-SCENES

The day we had to have Ollie's head shaved because his hair was coming out in massive clumps was extremely difficult. It was symbolic. While we told him he was going to be getting a short haircut, and he didn't care in the least, we knew it was because he was no longer going to have any hair. No hair on his head. No eyebrow hair. Likely no eyelashes. I tried very hard throughout this whole ordeal to not project my feelings of being scared or upset onto Ollie.

This day was no different, but I did let the tears stream down my face when they shaved his head. He couldn't see me as I was behind him. He was now essentially bald. I was letting myself mourn what was and what was yet to come.

Also, a note on the cost of medical care and medications. The special white blood cell medication that Ollie was prescribed to help his little body recover quicker was $7,000 a shot.

Yes, you read correctly. $7,000 for one shot.

Thankfully, we had, at this point, reached our deductible. Nonetheless, I was in disbelief when I heard it.

Our internal care team would, in the following months, work very closely with the manufacturer of this drug to procure it at the lowest cost possible. This often included utilizing coupons that they had for us and sitting on hold for hours to get it cleared.

I have no idea the extent of the total cost of Ollie's healthcare, but I would say an educated guess is in the seven figures.

November 24, 2021

Home—By the grace of God and our care team, we were able to make it home tonight about 8 p.m.!

Our nurse Kristen, who has been with us many days and nights at Cardinal Glennon, walked us out and gave me a big hug. She really helped keep the ball rolling yesterday and today, so we could make going home happen. This involved some big and little things both. To her, "Thank you" isn't enough. Your patience, kindness, compassion, and love for children and their families absolutely beam.

We told Ollie he would get to see the big Christmas tree in the lobby on the way out, and he absolutely loved it; also asking if Santa was there.

When we got outside, he said, "It's Christmas time out here," and "Those lights are so beautiful!" It was the sweetest thing. His mood instantly changed knowing that we were going home!

He loved looking at all the Christmas lights and decorations on our drive. It really is the little things, and seeing his eyes light up made my heart so full.

We are sending love from our home to yours for a restful, fun, and safe holiday. We are so glad to be back in our beds and the comfort of our space.

Prayers that Ollie can recover from this latest chemo infusion before we go back Tuesday for outpatient treatment.

Tomorrow marks thirty days since we found out this earth-shattering news and learned what Hepatoblastoma was.

I am grateful that we ended up at Cardinal Glennon that day and thankful beyond measure that they have been able to act so quickly to give Ollie the very best chance at a full recovery.

BEHIND-THE-SCENES

On November 16, after talking with several people about childcare options and ideas, including Ollie's daycare provider, we settled on trying an online platform to help us find a home care solution for Ollie. The posting had to be very specific about our situation to attract the right person. This is what I posted:

> *PT Nanny Needed for In-Home Care–Sunset Hills. Fun Child! Great Space! Excellent Pay! Flexibility!*
>
> *PT nanny for 3-year-old (2-3 days/Mon. & Thurs. + 1 or ½ day/16-24 hrs. in total). In-home, while we work from home. Contract would be a 6- month minimum with option for extension. Pay $20-25/hour.*
>
> *O. is a sweet, funny boy. Very communicative. Almost potty trained. He enjoys playgrounds, books, puzzles, art. He has previously attended a school, but was diagnosed with Hepatoblastoma (liver cancer) three weeks ago and will be undergoing treatment for the next several months. He has tolerated his first round of Chemo well with no sickness—just reduced energy and appetite.*
>
> *Job duties: play, provide some loose structure, art time and movement. Space: 4,000+ square foot home w/a dedicated playroom and finished basement and yard.*

Qualifications: Healthy, dependable, trustworthy.

Must be vaccinated for COVID and Flu. Early childhood/medical background desired.

On November 28, we received an application in response to our Care.com post from Kaitlin P. The email started, "I currently have a part-time position at Ranken Jordan Pediatric Hospital as a Therapy Technician. I have previously worked at Brain Balance Achievement Centers, so I have experience with special needs…"

I thought to myself, "Wow." This girl might be the answer to our prayers in looking for a special caregiver for Ollie.

We interviewed her online and then in person and felt strongly that she was the one. And we were right. Our prayers had been answered. Miss Kaitlin is the definition of a life angel. She showed up in ways both big and small for us throughout Ollie's journey, and to this day (2025), she still has a close relationship with Ollie and our family and watches him when we need help. He is also going to be in her wedding!

I will never forget just how special of a human Kaitlin is. An amazing detail of her personal faith journey is that in the year after meeting Ollie, she chose to get baptized.

Her testimonial was a testament to seeing God's love and grace work through Ollie. She felt called to God through Ollie, and it was amazing to see God find her. My life wish for Kaitlin is to know just how special of a human she is. I know she will be a wonderful wife and mother someday. We couldn't have endured our journey without her love and support. We hope to always stay close with her.

November 30, 2021

DAY 30 – ROUND-2. BRAVERY AND RESILIENCE.

I've been thinking a lot lately about bravery and resilience. How you cultivate it or how it cultivates you.

It is a little of both, I think.

It's a lifelong lesson and journey.

It often hurts, mentally, physically, and emotionally.

Sometimes it's easy, sometimes it's hard.

Sometimes it makes you beam with a sense of pride.

Sometimes it makes you cry.

An essential life skill.

What really amazes me is how Ollie knows things are different now, yet he doesn't ask what is going on. He knows and understands way more than he ever says.

He knows that he doesn't go to school anymore, that he must go to the hospital sometimes.

He knows he doesn't have hair anymore.

He knows he must wear a mask.

He knows he is hungry, but food tastes different and his belly feels weird.

He knows he has a big scar across his belly.

He knows he has a "button" on his chest (his port).

He knows he must take medicine sometimes, really a lot of times.

Through it all, Ollie has shown the utmost bravery and resiliency since day one.

It blows my mind, especially since we can't yet adequately explain what his diagnosis is to him. We also can't explain exactly what it is to be brave and resilient, but believe me, he knows.

From the moment he and I held hands in that x-ray room at urgent care, when in the darkness, the big, loud machine and sounds scared him, he chose to be brave. To have, in the very next few days, a CT scan, MRI, major surgery, and his first blood transfusion, and to try to walk with "tubie," he chose to be brave. Going from living at home to living ten days straight at a hospital, to taking numerous medications orally, to getting his head shaved, he chose to be brave. This kid is my hero. He rolled with it all.

How, just how, has this little boy, a mere two years old, decided he is going to accept this, most of the time, anyway? God is working through him. I can see it. He has absorbed it somehow. It's amazing to see just how courageous he is, day in and day out.

He had his Round-2, Week 2 infusion of chemo this a.m. Blood labs looked okay. His hemoglobin is low, and he will likely need a red blood transfusion on Friday when we are scheduled to be in anyway.

He also is low on magnesium and sulfates, so we are working on supplements so we don't have to have an IV at home. He didn't lose any weight.

The art therapist, Miss Bri, from Child Life Services, came and did art with Ollie, and he loved the stampers and special scissors she brought. Something fun and not scary made the time pass faster. Their laughter filled my heart with joy.

We will be back at Cardinal Glennon on Friday for his hearing benchmark test and ECHO screening to see if the treatment has done any damage, and to what extent.

Praying it hasn't or is minimal.

Monday, we go in for his MRI, CT and last chemo infusion for Round-2. Monday, December 6, is a big day for our care team to see the tumor and start to map out what steps are next in removing it or if further treatment is required.

Thank you again to each one of you for your continued messages, prayers, thoughts, cards, food, gift cards, toys, books, art supplies, puzzles, blankets, and other special gifts.

Everything is helping make our days easier and our hearts more at ease.

December 3, 2021

Hearing and heart tests.

Ollie made it through another marathon day at Cardinal Glennon like a champ.

We were due in at 8 a.m. for labs and to audiology by 8:45 a.m. He walked into the Costas Center and didn't get upset at all today, having his port accessed, vitals, blood drawn, and other basic screenings. In fact, he was just enjoying his show and even laughing and smiling from time to time.

The nurses commented on how good he was doing. It felt like a small win for him and all of us.

Next up was our audiology appointment, and he was so brave sitting on my lap, working through the hearing test in a very small soundproof room.

Of course, in true Cardinal Glennon style, they had a team working with us, one dedicated to helping him stay focused through games/toys and visuals.

After his hearing test, we went back to our room in the Costas Center, and Ollie requested vanilla yogurt. I am so relieved he is still eating a bit!

Another win.

Magnesium levels were lower than Tuesday, and phosphorus levels are low but stabilizing. Our doctor said he would need a magnesium drip today, given in the clinic via IV over four hours. It would also be her recommendation for us to go home with Ollie's port still accessed and learn how to administer IV fluids with these specific components over the weekend for twelve-hour blocks.

The alternative proposal was that he would need to be admitted to the hospital all weekend. So, we agreed that we would try the IV fluids at home.

Next up was his ECHO screening, and the lady conducting the sonography test was so awesome, helping calm his nerves and talking him through it.

Again, I can't overstate how nice it is that they speak and work with the kids at their levels. These people, their jobs and the technology absolutely amaze me. The machine literally shows us his heart chambers!

The magnesium took every bit of four hours, and Ollie had to be hooked up to the computer for vitals. Meaning he had to stay put.

He did great until about 2:30 p.m., the witching hour. We made it home at 4:30 p.m. just in time to grab the couriered medical solutions and supplies delivered to our front door and to greet the nurse who was going to teach us about how to do the IVs.

She was very patient and kind and went through all the steps in detail and then let us practice. She even helped us figure out how to hang his IV bag on his crib so that it would stay upright and be close enough to him overnight.

This process, like a lot of what we have gone through, was on the list of things we never thought we'd be doing or would want to do. But here we were. Learning. Stepping out of our comfort zone. Facing fears.

I'm proud of us.

Especially my husband, who helped calm me and convinced me it was going to be easier than we thought. Our nurse came at about 6:30 p.m. Brian and I got him up and running on his IV at about 7:15 p.m. in time for bed. Again, in Ollie form, he rolled with it. I told him Mom and Dad had to hook "tubie" up, and he simply said, "ok." Tomorrow we will disconnect for the day and reconnect at night again.

We are obviously exhausted tonight, but so incredibly grateful and relieved to report that the results of both the tests came back, and that no damage has occurred so far to his hearing or heart. Keep those prayers coming for more positive news on Monday with the MRI and CT.

BEHIND-THE-SCENES

It was around this time that I started to feel like a completely different human. Like a sort of shell of myself. Whenever we were home, I was having random panic attacks and thoughts that I was put on this planet to endure pain and that this pain I was feeling in heartache for Ollie was so difficult for me that I might not be able to live through it. My heart felt broken. I thought about dying. I thought about the living hell I was experiencing.

I knew it was awful to think this way, but the thoughts were there. How can anyone withstand this type of storm again, I thought? What if Ollie didn't make it? How could I live? While these thoughts were infrequent at first, whenever I had a few minutes to myself, they started to overtake my daily thoughts, and I knew I needed to get help as soon as possible. I couldn't manage the intensity of the situation on my own anymore.

I was still seeing my therapist, Dr. Therese, remotely via *FaceTime*, but conveying the severity of the situation was difficult.

She knew and encouraged me to call my general practitioner and speak to them about exactly how I was feeling.

The challenge was that I didn't want to risk going into the doctor's office because by putting myself in that environment, I could bring home germs or illnesses.

I called my general practitioner and explained the situation and what I was going through. I was asked to complete a test evaluating the severity of my depression and anxiety, and the result was conclusive. Ten out of ten that I would benefit from taking an antidepressant, Selective Serotonin Reuptake Inhibitors (SSRI). For me, Lexapro would be prescribed and be tremendously helpful in leveling off the waves of anxiety and depression I was feeling daily. I was grateful that I knew I should not be ashamed and ask for help. I needed it. The medication, combined with ongoing psychologist-based therapy, was another route for processing and acceptance.

December 6, 2021

DAY 35/36 – END OF ROUND-2 & SCANS.

Well, day thirty-five ended with another trip to the ER.

After an otherwise really nice day, including a special visit from one of Ollie's teachers at Lakeside Children's Academy, Mrs. Di, and her church brass band with carolers, Ollie started limping on late Sunday afternoon and spiked a fever of 101 plus.

We called to see what the on-call doctor for hematology at Cardinal Glennon suggested, and they said we needed to come into the ER. Ugh. We knew it, but were hoping to avoid another trip. After all, we were due in first thing Monday at 8 a.m.

The fever at that point is always a cause for concern. The on-call doctor in hematology calls the ER to let them know we and other oncology patients that are "followed" are coming, so his bracelet and information are ready to get us an ER room ASAP. That is reassuring.

Then they have one hour, protocol for "code sepsis" as they call it, to get a blood panel, other tests, and antibiotics in his bloodstream via his port. This time, they were especially concerned with the limp.

They ran some additional blood tests for "inflammation markers" and ordered an x-ray of his foot.

The orthopedic resident came and evaluated his foot, legs and joints from his foot to his hip. Blood test came back, and his white blood cell count was highly elevated. The inflammation markers also were elevated, but not overly concerning. Fever came down. They weren't entirely sure what was going. Since we were due back in the morning, Ollie wasn't considered neutropenic, low white blood cell count. We got to go home about 11 p.m.

Day 36, a bit tired and anxious, we arrived at the CG Costas center at 8 a.m.

We were lucky to get our same nurse, Mrs. Karen, that we had the first time Ollie had chemo, and the nurse who was with us all day last Friday for clinic. She collected Ollie's blood samples and got us on our way to imaging.

Mrs. Karen has been a nurse for forty-three years at Cardinal Glennon! She is obviously knowledgeable and so kind. It's nice to feel a sense of knowing with these wonderful people we are spending our days with. I tell Ollie they are his "special helpers."

In imaging, we were in the same waiting/prep room we were in for his first MRI. It did bring back some memories for us all. The uncertainty, the reality.

On the sliding door, the nurses write in erasable marker the child's initials, age and orders. For me, it's difficult to look at, "O.G. 2yrs, MRI/CT".

Just the unbelievable nature of it all. Still! How?

The anesthesiologist came in and explained that Ollie would be under general anesthesia with a breathing tube for the procedures.

They were able to give him a sedative via his port before so he wouldn't have as much separation anxiety from us as we had to hand him off to the team. He went in with his blanket, Ollie Bear and Big Mickey.

Brian and I went to get a pager so we could know when he was done in about two hours, and to get a coffee at the kiosk in the lobby, and then headed to the Ronald McDonald House on the Fifth Floor for some quiet time and a space to work.

This space is so nice for families. We are grateful for it. A little past noon, our pager rang, and we went down to his recovery room. He woke up within an hour, and we headed back to Costas for his last chemo for Round-2.

Ollie was very hungry when he woke up. He didn't get his normal food intake yesterday due to the ER visit, and then couldn't eat this a.m. He wanted more vanilla yogurt, so Mrs. Karen got him that and some homemade chocolate chip cookies.

I was so happy he wanted to eat. He got settled in and, after a few outbursts, due, we think, to being super tired and hungry and yes, being back at the hospital again, he was able to get his chemo.

Our nurses let us know that he would need to be on the at-home IV for the rest of the week due to his magnesium and phosphorus levels still not being met.

His white blood cell count did drop from seventeen on Sunday evening to thirteen today. No fever, and the rest of his panel looked okay. We were okay to go home.

Our doctor would be calling us with the preliminary results of the scans. We were anxious.

Results: Dr. Lauren started with the good news, and my heart immediately sank, just intuitively. But good news is still good news, so let's hear it.

His tumor did shrink. Not a lot, but some, and it is her belief that it hasn't shrunk more because some of what is being measured is dead tissue, based on the positive AFP results a few weeks back.

The other good news, the tumor has not spread.

What threw us a curveball was what she characterized as how the tumor is interacting with the Inferior Vena Cava (IVC) vein. The IVC is a large vein that carries deoxygenated blood from the lower body back to the heart. It's the largest vein in the human body and plays a critical role in circulation.

Ollie's first scans showed the tumor pushed up into this area, and it was thought that the tumor was separate from the IVC.

Now, the new images, which show a better picture, because the tumor has shrunk, indicate there may be some level of "involvement" with the IVC vein and the tumor.

To what extent, if any, we don't know yet.

If this is true, options for resection become more limited, but still can occur, and the transplant team would likely become involved.

We are not there yet, but we should know more as the week progresses and the different specialties look at Ollie's images. His case will be presented to the Cardinal Glennon tumor board on Thursday.

We meet with a surgeon at Children's Hospital this week and our Cardinal Glennon Surgeon next Monday. It's a lot to process, and we are trying to focus on the good and not go into the hole of worry for the unknown until we know more.

Through tears, I did tell our doctor I was grateful for more information for our team so they can hopefully find the best course of action for curing our son from this horrible disease.

We are hanging in there.

Hanging onto the small moments of joy and light that bring us smiles amidst the many overwhelming hours.

Ollie is still in great spirits, mostly, and just amazes us in terms of resilience and strength. What a boy. How this experience is going to shape his life is yet to be determined, but I know that we will all come out different and stronger because of it.

Keep the prayers coming for patience, clarity, solutions, comfort, healing, strength, and of course, grace.

December 7, 2021 (A.M.)

DAY 37. BACK AT 4N.

Day 36 ended the same as day thirty-five with another trip to the ER due to strange fever spikes in the afternoon/evening.

More tests and antibiotics. This time, they decided to admit us.

While Ollie's fever dropped again, his heart rate was a bit elevated. We got to the ER about 7 p.m. and finally to our room at 1 a.m.

We are beyond exhausted, frustrated, and concerned. It's been a tough 48-plus hours.

We are fueling on hope and lots of coffee; Ollie on vanilla yogurt, art, Daniel Tiger, and Mickey.

We are keeping each other in as best of company as we can. He is in good spirits and still rolling with it. Tired, but completely expected.

Not sure what the plan is for the day. They want to continue to observe him. Good news is all his blood panels came back normal-ish, and tests for bacterial and viral infection negative.

They are trying to figure out if the fever spikes are his body's response to the new white blood cell medication that he is on to help him recover from chemo, or just his response to the chemo in general.

We are taking lots of deep breaths and trying our best to be patient as we progress through this.

I know you are all praying. We feel it. Thank you.

December 7, 2021 (P.M.)

We made it home! We will continue to closely monitor Ollie this week for fevers and keep him on his evening at-home IVs for fluids and key electrolytes.

We have two upcoming appointments with surgeons in the next few days, and then we will be due back to check in for inpatient chemo Round-3, one week from today.

This will set him up to be done with Round-3 by the end of this month. Rest, shower, nourishment and a little downtime will do us all wonders.

I ordered Ollie a mini-Christmas tree and some kid ornaments a few days ago for him to decorate his own tree in his room at home. It was so nice tonight to see him enjoying a moment of the season while decorating it.

December 9, 2021

A good day with more blood.

We had an appointment at Cardinal Glennon today for his labs to evaluate if he needed to stay on the at-home overnight IVs, if so, they would have to change his port needle which is only good for one week.

His hemoglobin has been right in line for another transfusion for about a week or so, and they decided he should have a red blood cell transfusion today. Each time they bring a bag of blood in, and he has had to have numerous transfusions in seven weeks, I am so grateful and, honestly, amazed. The difference the blood makes is something you can visibly see take an immediate effect.

I put a note on Facebook, but I'll say it here again. Please, if you can donate, consider giving blood or platelets. The American Red Cross makes it so easy.

After another five hours, this child did good, having to stay put again. We were out! Port got to come out, and he is off the IVs for the weekend.

He did get to pick two toys from the toy closet, which has toys donated from Friends of Kids with Cancer, and that really brightened his spirits.

These organizations and those who help fundraise and facilitate their services are essential for the support of families going through the trauma of a diagnosis such as this.

His first request? To head to the park. So that we did!

After the week we have had, it was so nice to see him running around playing in nature at the park. He doesn't play as long anymore, but he was happy to climb, slide and swing. We had a neighbor bring us a delicious dinner, and we were all able to relax a bit tonight. He even said, "I'm having so much fun." I have hardly heard him verbalize that feeling since this all started.

Small wins.

His Round-3 treatment got moved from Tuesday check-in to Monday, December 13, since we will be there meeting with the pediatric surgeon anyways.

We will hope to be out Wednesday.

We are anxious to have to spend more nights at the hospital. It's hard to communicate this plan to a two-year-old. He has started saying, "I don't want to be here." I mean, who can blame him?

It is, at this point, the consensus of the team that he will likely need Round-3 and Round-4 of chemo before we will know his route, meaning, safe resection, more chemo, or a potential transplant.

These next two rounds are "critical". Please keep praying for shrinkage, minimal side effects, sustained energy, and patience for us all.

CHAPTER 8

THIRD ROUND

December 13, 2021

DAY 43 – ROUND-3, DAY 1. "THE ONLY WAY OUT IS THROUGH."
As we prepared our hospital bags for our planned readmission today, Brian and I felt anxious.

Honestly, these words are still quite daunting at this point, but we are trying to make the best of this challenging situation we are all in.

We know it's important that we both stay strong and positive for Ollie and each other. But we also know that the middle, where we are at now, is often the hardest.

We have, most likely, six more weeks of chemo before a surgery occurs; Round-3 and Round-4. Then an additional six weeks; Round-5 and Round-6 of chemo after surgery.

Also, it is weighing heavy on us that it is still unknown if the tumor can come out successfully.

We will know more after this third treatment round, which started today.

In three weeks, the scans that were completed last week will be completed with the addition of a triple-phase CT scan to look more specifically at the veins and arteries of his liver.

Short story: the tumor must shrink more and in key areas.

Within the last week, we have met with two very skilled and knowledgeable pediatric surgeons. One is the original surgeon who completed Ollie's emergency biopsy the week we found out about his diagnosis. The other does similar work at Children's Hospital in Saint Louis. Their takeaways from the new MRI and CT scans completed last week were: a) the tumor shrunk but not enough to take it out yet; b) the tumor's proximity to the portal vein is still, at this time, problematic; c) IVC vein does not overly concern them yet.

We have also been introduced to the organ transplant team, should we need them. Yes, this is as overwhelming as it sounds from a mental standpoint. This involved additional blood work taken today and meeting with one of the transplant surgeons and lead nurses. This path is most certainly scarier and riskier, but also an option should we need it.

We are grateful for options, so I am reminding myself of that through the discussions.

Over the next three weeks, this team will prepare everything to list Ollie on the donor list should that be needed. It is our understanding that he would be listed high on the national list based on his diagnosis in grouping position 1B, primarily reserved for very sick pediatric patients under 12 who meet specific urgency criteria.

Cardinal Glennon does not use living donors for pediatrics at this point, so we would wait for a deceased donor, one ideally close to his size.

We obviously are just starting to digest this information to better understand what this path looks like if he needs a transplant to survive this.

The good news is his AFP is down to 2700 from 16000 from his original number of 55000 plus. Still high but going in the right direction towards a healthy number of less than ten. Also, his spirits are great!

Thank you, God, for Ollie's sweet disposition, understanding, and tolerance for all the time we must spend sitting, hooked up to "tubie."

We have been keeping busy with books, art projects, games, and his TV shows. The days are long. We have been here for eight hours already and were just able to start the first of five chemo's.

A lot of the time leading up to the start is hydration and pre-meds for nausea. The Cisplatin will run now for six hours, followed by the others over the night and into tomorrow.

So many emotions.

This is the reality of the middle, where we are. Seven weeks into this nightmare. And as I told Brian on Thursday, as we were leaving Cardinal Glennon for the fourth time last week, no matter what, we will all get through this. One way or another.

Focusing on one day at a time is key.

That is easier said than done. The constant uncertainty is hard to sit with. Extra prayers for us, please.

The tumor's response to Round-3 of treatment will be crucial to determining Ollie's path forward through his cancer diagnosis.

At this point in the treatment process, we had to really continue to lean into the uncertainty and not think too far out. Minute by minute.

It was also very important to not lock in on one particular outcome preference. I knew from experience that I had to keep space for the possibility of anything happening.

"Anything" could mean Ollie would be cured, in full remission. He could potentially need a transplant. Or worse, his body not be able to continue to respond to the chemo and be overtaken by the cancer.

The days were long at the hospital, and we really had to focus on the little bits of light to get through it.

Thankfully, Ollie really managed all of it well. We tried our best to keep him busy, which also kept us busy. The Child Life Services that I frequently mention were key to keeping us all happy and sane.

December 14, 2021

ROUND-3, DAY 2.

Day 2 started with a lot of nausea very early for our sweet Ollie after more chemo throughout the night.

We were able to get it under control, and he slept until 8:30 a.m. or so. He requested to get out and walk around the floor a bit about 9:30 a.m., and that was so great for all of us.

He was then set up for an intravenous immunoglobulin (IVIG) to increase his immunoglobulin at 10 a.m. That took a couple hours.

While he was getting the IVIG, we had lots of visitors, including the hospital Chaplain, Madison, and our favorite resident, Meredith.

The transplant team pharmacist also came to introduce himself and talk about typical prescriptions should Ollie need a transplant. Ms. Deb, the sweet staff psychologist, came by with a play medical set for Ollie to practice being doctor and nurse on his stuffies and us. He really liked that!

The heart team then followed with an EKG and a lot of body stickers!

And following that, additional anti-bacteria meds, his last protectant drug, and final chemo at 6 p.m. A lot goes on during these days. Our amazing care team got us out at 7:30 p.m. tonight.

Thank you to our nurses Lindsay, Maddy, and Kristen, who over the course of the last thirty-six hours helped keep things moving along and took gentle care of our boy and our spirits.

Maddy and Kristen have been our primary nurses throughout. You all make this so much easier on us. Your kind, sweet, and caring dispositions are treasured, especially during these long, stressful days and nights.

We also learned how to administer his white blood cell shot, so we didn't have to stay an extra twenty-four hours. That will be given tomorrow. He is on overnight IV fluids at home again, which will help his recovery. We are so glad to have only had to stay one night! We will pray for rest and recovery the next few days.

We are due back Friday for labs, hoping and praying not before. Hugs from all of us to you.

BEHIND-THE-SCENES

When we were in the middle of Oliver's chemo treatments, it was winter. The cold, dark, and dreary December, January, and February days and nights.

When we were home from the hospital, at night, I would purposely step outside to slowly walk to the mailbox, just to soak in the quiet, stillness of the night and breathe in the cold, crisp air.

It was so therapeutic. I would look up at the night sky.

I would see the stars and the moon glowing so bright, sharing their magnificent light, which was magnified in the darkness.

I would pause in the stillness, breathing deep the air, just staring in amazement at the bright light. It was always something about the moon that was tremendously soothing. It could be just a spec, a half, or a full-on glow. It reminded me that something much bigger was at play in this universe. It was one of these cold and dark nights that I was also visited by a Thunderbird. Not literally, but figuratively, in a book I was reading about angels and signs.

To most people, this would mean absolutely nothing, but to me, it meant everything. It was a sign from my guardian angels, an ancestral visit.

For a few years I had been tuning into energy fields, being more compelled than ever to listen to the universe, my God, and the quiet whispers. Part of this was in observing the personal experience of a good friend, Meredith, who had become a Reiki Master. One of these nights, I was sitting on the floor outside Ollie's room waiting for him to fall asleep so I could help Brian position his IV bag on his crib. It was a two-person job to get it positioned correctly. It was finally quiet for a moment, and I was contemplating. It had been the most surreal, stressful, and terrifying month and a half of my life.

It was about 7:45 p.m. and I had a dark blue hardcover book titled "*A Little Bit of Angels*" in my hand. I had coincidentally picked this book up a month or so before Ollie's diagnosis in this bookstore in Old Town, Saint Charles, Missouri. My lifelong friend Angie and I had spent the day there, having brunch and shopping when she was in town visiting from Minnesota. Just before I opened it, I received a random text message from my dear friend Meredith, the Reiki Master.

Meredith was out shopping and said she was thinking of me, and looked up and saw a handwritten note on a shelf. She snapped a photo of the note and sent it.

I received it and was stunned. In that exact moment, I was holding a book on just the topic, angels. What are the chances? I then closed my eyes and meditated. I asked God for the message I was supposed to receive. I then randomly opened my angel book to a page that literally took my breath away.

Pages fifty and fifty-one provided a creative visual mediation to work with the angels that reside within you. The angel fact that was referenced was the Native American Thunderbird. To me, this was a very specific message from my ancestors. Let me explain more.

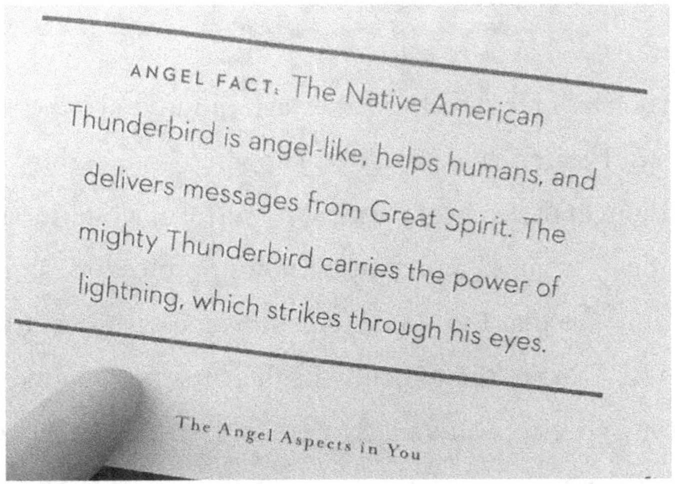

A few days prior, I was tidying up my office and found a very old photograph of my paternal grandparents, circa August 1963. It was tucked away in this old antique cigar tin that I had on my footrest that served as a coffee table.

It was one of those four by four black and white photos and had a cursive handwritten note on the back in red ink, "At Sioux Narrows." It was my grandparents, Evelyn and George Gray, standing in front of a Native American totem pole with a Thunderbird atop it.

As soon as I received these messages, I ran down the stairs to get the photo. I stared at it. I started googling "thunderbird meaning": "Often thought of as one of the most powerful of all spirits, a supernatural being—a symbol representing power, protection, and strength." I was so in awe that I was able to get this message, and I felt a sense of renewal. Despite the difficulty of the situation I found myself in, I knew my ancestors and angels were with me, and they wanted me to know. Meredith was the conduit for this message transfer in that moment. It was incredible and something I will never forget.

December 20, 2021

Six whole nights home since our last admit. If you want your bed to feel like a million bucks, sleep at a hospital for a night or two.

Ollie has been doing well by all accounts, except for eating enough. This is to be expected, though. The chemo has that effect in general. We had a quick appointment last Friday to check his vitals and labs, and everything looked okay, but he had to stay on his overnight IVs that have added magnesium and phosphorus. We are all relatively used to the process now.

Ollie knows that "tubie" takes a drink at night–the saline flush first, which he likes to "help" with, and then the tube/pump gets connected and stays with him overnight, strapped onto his crib.

Regarding the eating, our doctor spoke with us about the likelihood of putting him on a feeding tube through his nose in the coming weeks.

We are trying everything, but getting a two-year-old to do anything he doesn't want to is quite impossible. Especially eating.

Our medical team is closely watching his weight, which has dropped to the fifth percentile. If this continues, the feeding tube is the next step. It's again one of those things that at this moment sounds scary, but if it will help him, we will absolutely do it. Anything to get him through.

We were so thankful for no random fevers over the past few days. We did start him on an antihistamine to help with inflammation in his bone joints from the white blood cell medication he is on. Both seem to help his general recovery.

His energy has been impressive. It's so great to see him happy and running around as a toddler would. Most days he requests to go to Suson Park to feed the chickens and goats and to play a bit on the playground. He especially loves the swings. Today he was extra sweet with the mini horse and donkeys. The power of nature in his healing journey should not be understated.

Brian and I were able to go on a quick, much-needed date on Friday night thanks to Mom and Dad Geen.

We are beyond grateful they live so close and are the kind, compassionate, helpful, and loving people they are. We couldn't do this without them or their unwavering support and faith.

Today, our part-time nanny, Miss Kaitlin, started. She is a fourth-year college student studying recreational therapy and currently works at a local pediatric bridge hospital.

Ollie was thrilled to have someone else to play with besides Mom and Dad. Grandma has been graciously helping, too. Brian and I were also happy to have some time to ourselves to work.

It was a process to find her; someone to introduce into our delicate situation and home in the middle of a pandemic, but we are hoping it works out perfect for both her and Ollie.

Tomorrow, we have Round-3, day 7 of treatment. A possible blood transfusion, depending on his levels. We are happy to continue to progress down the treatment path, but it's also so hard to see him doing well, to know he has to get hit with the chemo drugs again. Ugh.

Sweet boy. You are a warrior.

I find myself wishing often that we were through this Round and not just in the murky middle. This week and next week we have outpatient treatment and then more scans to follow.

Praying so hard that this tumor moves away from the critical artery/vein area, and we have good news that it can come out after Round-4 in January. The transplant team will be ready to list him ASAP if not. We are making the best out of our days and the warm weather when it presents itself! Thank you for your continued thoughts, prayers, and support.

BEHIND-THE-SCENES

The key to staying positive in the murky middle was to constantly remind myself to not think too much ahead. I have said this many times throughout the process, but I cannot overstate this. Managing expectations, one day, one hour at a time.

This advice applies to many stressful situations you may find yourself in life.

And that was the crazy thing about "time" at this point: it seemed to stand still. The days were slow. I think now, what a blessing that truly was.

We just were there being. There was no doing, just being and waiting.

December 21, 2021

ROUND-3, DAY 7.

Outpatient chemo treatment.

Morning started out with Ollie saying, "I'm hungry," as we got him out of bed. He ate strawberries, turkey sausage, and a waffle with peanut butter for breakfast and ate it all.

We had a special delivery of the cutest gingerbread train.

He played and was in great spirits. We didn't tell him that we had to go anywhere, but when he saw Brian packing his computer bag, he blurted out, "I don't want to go to the hospital."

He just knew.

We told him very calmly that we only had to go for a little bit to have his "tubie" looked at and to give "tubie" medicine, and then we would be home.

He then said, "Okay, I go see the double-decker bus." I told him yes; the double-decker bus is at Cardinal Glennon. That is what the hospital is called.

We haven't yet called the hospital much by name, but I am starting to feel like we can. Also, he believes that "tubie" is separate from him, and if "tubie" takes the medicine, he is not.

It is working for now.

Weight was okay today. Up a little! A definite win.

Thank God. No feeding tube needed yet.

Vitals, labs, some waiting.

We will all be professionals by the end of this!

He does good for the first few hours, then lately has had some major breakdowns about two-three hours in. We are working through it. It's the anxiety and stress of not wanting to be there.

We were able to talk with Ollie's doctor for a bit. I can't emphasize enough how wonderful she is. Based on his labs, she is keeping him on the overnight IVs, and we agreed, they are absolutely helping. He got his quick chemo infusion, and we were out in four hours!

He did, of course, request to go to the park on the way home, but fell asleep on the way there.

We were glad to have him rest! And for some quiet time for us, too.

Last infusion for Round-3 is Tuesday, December 28. On January 4, we have been scheduled to start Round-4, inpatient. This is also the same week scans have been scheduled. We are going to try our best to enjoy the coming days and look forward to Santa visiting our house on Thursday. Ollie's school helped coordinate.

December 23, 2021

DAY 58. CHRISTMAS MAGIC

What an incredible day we had.

It has been what feels like so long since we have been able to say that.

All the stars aligned today.

Ollie felt good, and our Lakeside Children's Academy family arranged to have Santa make a special visit to our house!

Double vaccinated, boosted, and masked, Santa, Mrs. Sue, and Mrs. Laura were able to come in our house for a private visit. We also have a medical-grade air cleaner.

Ollie loved it, seeing him be able to be a normal toddler for a few minutes was so incredibly heartwarming. It was exactly what we all needed.

After our visit with Santa, we were able to visit Ollie's favorite place, Suson Park, to see the animals, and then stop for a visit at Grandpa and Grandma Geen's.

Ollie was so happy to be at their house again and to see their special Christmas decorations, and we were even able to do a family walk around the subdivision lake since it was sixty-three degrees! Talk about feeling normal again for all of us.

It's hard for me to articulate how we are filled in our hearts with gratitude for the continued outpouring of kindness, generosity, support, and love. "Thank you" does not suffice. It truly doesn't seem adequate.

Please know, each one of you who has and continues to reach out with notes and messages of support and love; prayers, mass devotions, candle devotions, delicious meals, gift cards, books, art supplies, creative activities to help us pass the time; we feel your love, and these gestures are beyond anything we could ever think.

Just wow!

Also, the donations from our tribe to both Cardinal Glennon and Friends of Kids with Cancer now total $3,300 plus. Absolutely incredible. A blood drive in Ollie's honor will also be hosted by the Red Cross and Lakeside Children's Academy sometime in February 2022!

We never in a million years would have thought this would be a journey we would be faced with, but let me tell you, having the continued support of family, friends, friends of family and friends, and total strangers is the most humbling experience of our life.

We will never forget it and most certainly pay it forward when we are through this.

I am taking lots of pictures of everything, along with purposefully documenting on this blog site. I want Ollie to know later in life why we call him "Warrior," what he went through, and just exactly how many people were supporting and lifting us through this time.

Merry Christmas with love.

December 25, 2021

DAY 60. MERRY CHRISTMAS

We have been home since our last admit, eleven whole nights now, and so grateful to make it through the holiday without any unplanned visits to Cardinal Glennon.

We have, of course, been playing it very safe and staying home or playing outside. Ollie has had some good days. We are incredibly impressed with his overall energy, and his eating has really picked up this week. The overnight IV fluids also seem like they are helping tremendously.

And the weather has felt like Spring. Good for everyone! Next outpatient chemo infusion is Tuesday, December 28, to finish Round-3. Here's to making it to Tuesday with continued strength and renewed hope.

We have had as nice of a Christmas as we could have under the circumstances, and thank everyone for their messages, gifts, prayers, and continued thoughts as we navigate through this time.

December 28, 2021

DAY 63. ROUND-3, DAY 15!

Ollie has completed Round-3 of his chemo treatment. Thank you, God.

This technically marks halfway through his standard chemo treatment protocol, which allows for six rounds; four before surgery, two after.

We had a relatively short visit to Cardinal Glennon today. In and out in three hours! Ollie's weight has stabilized for now, and his blood counts looked good.

We will keep him on his overnight IV infusions for hydration and the added phosphorus and magnesium. Next visit is first thing Tuesday, January 4, for inpatient scans and start of Round-4.

All our patience is being tried daily, but we are working on it. One day at a time. Most days it's one hour at a time. It is hard with the pandemic virus variant cases rapidly increasing to consider taking our immunocompromised sweet boy anywhere, even with a mask. Anxiety-inducing is an understatement.

He is feeling stir crazy. Definitely a trying time for all of us. I saw a sign last week that spoke to the situation:

"God's Timing Might Be Sooner Than You Think. Be Patient."

I added it to our family picture wall.

BEHIND-THE-SCENES

The holidays, both Thanksgiving and Christmas, were very isolating for us that year.

We obviously were so grateful to not be in the hospital. But being at home with our toddler who had cancer was also very bittersweet. We really couldn't see any people directly because the risk of getting

COVID was so great. We didn't want to risk Ollie contracting it and ending up spending more unplanned days in the hospital.

I know this was also hard on our family and friends, but they understood.

The creative alternative was they would do a drive-by to drop off meals, treats, gifts, and wine, and to put up various holiday yard décor.

They would roll down their car windows and wave, and if we were able to talk, we would stay ten feet or so away. It was such a strange time. We did the best we could to make it as special as we could for Ollie and ourselves, but it was all just so weird.

We will never forget the two very special visits that were coordinated by Ollie's daycare; the private Santa visit and a visit from the Salvation Army brass band and carolers.

Both experiences felt like absolute magic and amplified light in our darkness. A big thank you, Mrs. Sue, Mrs. Laura, and Mrs. Di. God's hand was and continues to work through each of you.

CHAPTER 9

FOURTH ROUND

January 4, 2022

DAY 70. ROUND-4, DAY 1.

What a day.

It started with arriving at Cardinal Glennon at 6:45 a.m. for his scheduled CT scan. The sedation and bringing him into the scan room never gets easier.

The machine is so large and intimidating. But I am grateful for technology and the wonderful staff caring for him. And we are so ready to see if the chemo is doing what it is supposed to be doing.

He woke up from his sedation very unhappy, and it persisted for a good hour and a half. He wanted to go home and not to the Costas Center.

We were finally able to get him calm down with some anti-anxiety meds and music therapy. Thank you, Ms. Kelly!

Labs were drawn and indicated he needed a red blood cell transfusion.

While that was being ordered, our doctor came into our room quite concerned with what the radiologist saw on the CT scan.

She thought there might be a blood clot in the IVC vein. He would need to go immediately to get an ultrasound for additional investigation.

We took some deep breaths.

Brian took our overnight bags up to our room on 4N to check in, and I took Ollie to get the ultrasound. I was incredibly nervous.

But in true Ollie fashion, he did so well, lying still, for the most part, while the tech and radiologist both did an extensive look at the IVC vein from his liver to his knees.

It was interesting. It was stressful. I was trying to stay calm, but I really started to feel overwhelmed and anxious.

The most amazing news followed. He does not have a blood clot, and the tumor has shrunk! The radiologist did not elaborate, but we would know more soon. We are praying the shrinkage is in the areas of most concern near the major blood vessels.

The blood flow is slower in the IVC vein area because it is being pushed by the tumor. Now that the tumor has receded a bit, they are able to see a clearer picture of the area.

We got up to our room about 1:30 p.m., and Ollie had another special visit from the art therapist, Ms. Bri. He loved his time with her.

We learned from Ms. Bri that her job is partly funded through the hospital and partly through the Friends of Kids with Cancer organization. These therapists are just so essential to the kids' mental health, and they give the parents a few minutes of respite too.

Blood transfusion started about 3 p.m.

Before each transfusion, they run a type screen to ensure his blood type hasn't changed due to all the infusions. Still O+.

We got a special delivery to our room during all this; not one, but two special Build-A-Bears from a colleague of mine, which included a heartwarming and encouraging note. It was so kind, unexpected, and really lifted all our spirits. "Thank you, Jason and family, who know all too well what it's like to have a child with a complex medication condition."

We heard from our doctor that the preliminary review of the scans would indicate we are moving in the right direction, but the surgeons still needed to weigh in.

Tomorrow, late afternoon, the Tumor Board meets and Ollie's case will get reviewed. We will get additional feedback after that, along with new AFP levels.

Chemo finally started at 8 p.m. tonight.

Whew.

The Cisplatin runs for six hours, followed by the four other chemo drugs. Ollie is strong, resilient, and the absolute bravest. We are praying the chemo infusion goes okay over the next day and that we hear additional positive news. Keep those prayers coming. We feel them and know they are working!

BEHIND-THE-SCENES

Speaking of blood, Ollie's school, Lakeside Children's Academy, in conjunction with the American Red Cross, will host a blood drive in Ollie's honor on February 5, 2022. This drive will be held at the Daniel Boone Public Library in Ellisville.

Your blood donation will be meaningful to us and so many others.

January 6, 2022

DAY 72. ROUND-4, DAY 3.

We can breathe!

Day 2 ended with Ollie's oncology doctor presenting his case and new scans at the Cardinal Glennon Tumor Board. She had told us Tuesday that the new scans indicated we were "headed in the right direction." His tumor shrank, but she wanted to speak with the other disciplines to get their perspectives on the approach; especially the surgeon; on resect versus transplant.

At 4:30 p.m., our phone rang, and I put her on speaker. Anxious, Brian and I sat together on the couch to hear her report. Ollie's AFP cancer blood marker is down to 815. This was more than she was expecting and very good news!

When we were originally admitted at his diagnosis, this number was 55,000+. It has, since treatment, been progressively falling.

His last test of this was three weeks ago, and it was a little over 2,000.

A healthy number is less than 10. So, it still has a way to go but getting much closer! This is a number they will closely monitor as he progresses through recovery and for years following.

Next, she said, "His tumor has shrunk substantially." We both felt an immediate sense of relief, like we could breathe again.

When we asked by how much, she told us the new dimensions, and it is now roughly half the size it originally was!

Importantly, the surgery team feels like it can be successfully resected. It will be a joint surgery with the transplant team also there to assist with another set of eyes.

Our doctor has requested his surgery be set for the week of January 31, or at the latest, the week of February 7.

Timing is important for several reasons. Ollie can't be off chemo too long. And we need to save two rounds of the chemo protocol for after his surgery. This is to ensure no cancer cells remain in his body.

We will be discharged today and back Tuesday, January 11, and the following week Tuesday, January 18, for outpatient chemo to finish Round-4. A new MRI and CT will be completed the week of January 24th for final planning. In the meantime, they are putting him on eighteen-hour fluids to keep his hydration and key electrolytes where they need to be.

The chemo he is on is very hard on his kidneys, so they watch the magnesium and phosphorus closely. He needs more of both now, as his little body has had to withstand additional drugs as each round is additive.

It will be challenging only having six hours a day off from "tubie" but hopefully, it is only for the short term!

This is actually a small win because they had originally told us twenty-four-hour fluids, and we had advocated that he needed some time off to be free and move around.

All in all, we are feeling extremely relieved, grateful, and hopeful that Ollie will be able to avoid transplant and have this tumor taken out soon.

He has, over the past three weeks, been a lot like his normal, playful, sweet self. He is eating better, more energy, dancing! We thought that the added fluids were potently helping stabilize his energy levels. I still think that is true, however, his tumor is shrinking, and he is likely feeling better, too.

Keep all your prayers coming; we appreciate each one.

January 11, 2022

DAY 77. ROUND-4, DAY 8.

A visit to Costas Center today for outpatient chemo, anti-bacterial medicine for his lungs, and a port change.

Labs looked good; electrolytes have finally stabilized! We have been chasing that for a while.

He will still have to stay on the eighteen-hour IV each day at home so that his overall kidney function continues to improve.

It's challenging because the bag is heavy and rolling it around on a stand isn't really feasible for a 3-year-old, but we just stay close and help him pick it up to move it as he moves.

Ollie turned three on Sunday.

We were able to celebrate with Grandpa and Grandma Geen with some pizza and cake.

Ollie had fun looking at his decorations, balloons, and opening his many presents.

Mostly we were so thankful to be home celebrating together and not at the hospital.

Today we learned his surgery will most likely be February 2. We have another chemo infusion next Tuesday, January 18.

On January 24, he will have another MRI and CT and hearing/heart tests. We will meet with the surgeon on January 31.

Ollie's Blood Drive, sponsored by Lakeside Children's Academy, in conjunction with the Red Cross, will be on Saturday, February 5, 2022, at the Daniel Boone Library Branch in Ellisville. No walk-ins will be allowed, and sign-up will be first-come, first-served. Please give blood!

I'll share sign-up information once I have it. We are hoping to fill fifty to sixty spots!

We are praying to stay healthy and especially pandemic virus-free over the next few weeks. The state of the current pandemic variant has us extremely nervous.

BEHIND THE SCENES

In the middle of this ordeal, Ollie turned three on January 9, 2022. I remember thinking we had to make this birthday extra special. I mean, what if it was his last birthday, our last time to celebrate with him? I ordered him a special birthday shirt, a Mickey cake from a local bakery, and had some large helium balloons made to pick up from a local party supply store. The balloons were a traditional number three and a Mickey Mouse with a star that you could customize with your own personal message made of letter stickers. On one side, I spelled out "Brave Warrior," and on the other, "Ollie."

We had a mini photo shoot with noise makers, and he couldn't have been more excited. As I was taking the photos, I couldn't help but notice just how fragile he looked. He was clearly very sick and weak.

What a fighter. I hoped and prayed that this wouldn't be his last birthday with us, but if it was, we were going to make it as memorable as we could. We wanted him to have as much fun as his body would allow, and I wanted to document it.

Simultaneously, we were dealing with a tremendous amount of uncertainty and stress regarding his overall path forward. We were carefully considering Ollie's options by meeting with different hospitals and surgeons for his high-risk, complicated liver resection surgery.

It felt like the weight of the world was on our shoulders.

There was so much to consider, and the chosen surgeon's specialized approach could mean the stark difference between remission and recurrence.

January 18, 2022

DAY 84. ROUND-4, DAY 15. TODAY WAS A GOOD DAY!

All of Ollie's numbers looked great, so he only had to get his chemo infusion. The last infusion for Round-4.

We are also so glad to report that until at least Friday, he gets to be completely off his at-home IVs! We will get his numbers rechecked on Friday.

A break for him and us! He will really enjoy not being so restricted from 3 p.m. to 9 a.m. and being able to have a normal bath instead of a sponge bath. It is truly the little things!

We have been grateful for help from our new part-time nanny, Kaitlin, and Grandma Anna. We couldn't do this without them! New scans on Monday, triple phase MRI and CT for final surgery prep. They will also check blood counts to see if he needs another blood transfusion.

We meet with the surgeon from Children's Hospital on January 27 and the Cardinal Glennon surgeon on January 31. Surgery is tentatively scheduled for February 2.

Mark your calendar and sign up to give blood in Ollie's Honor! Coordinated by the Red Cross in conjunction with Ollie's school, Lakeside Children's Academy on Saturday, February 5, 2022, from 11 a.m.-3 p.m. at the Daniel Boone Library Branch in Ellisville (300 Clarkson Rd., Ellisville, Missouri 63011). Appointments are through the Red Cross.

January 23, 2022

DAY 89. HOPE WINS.

It's been a day of subtle, unexpected reminders from the universe. It started with Ollie requesting to play at Des Peres Park; playing, laughing, talking; really enjoying himself for over an hour!

Running around. Climbing. Going down slides.

He was so incredibly active. The most we have seen in a long time.

Des Peres Park is hard for me. It is where Ollie fell—an actual blessing—and which ultimately revealed to us three days later, his tumor and cancer diagnosis.

It is also a place I worked for five-plus years. The park is adjacent to City Hall. The irony is heavy. On our walk back to the car, the car parked next to us had a bumper sticker that simply said, "Hope Wins." I took a picture. I knew God was reminding me.

We have been making the most of Ollie's time off the IV. It has been such a nice break. In a lot of ways, we have started to feel somewhat normal again. We don't have to keep a strict schedule of when we are able to leave the house. Ollie can roam and play as a normal toddler would; he can take a bath, he doesn't have to have the bag strapped to his crib. He is sleeping better and doesn't wake up all wet from the constant infusion of fluids.

We also haven't had to change his sheets every single day.

All the little things that really add up to making life right now a bit easier. We have had friends and family spend time cooking and delivering us delicious meals. We have friends and family all over the country sending us pictures of themselves donating blood. For many, it is a first time! And, many people have signed up to donate at Ollie's Blood Drive on February 5, 2022.

Brian and I got to go out on a date!

We receive messages and calls daily, of prayers, thoughts, support, and encouragement. People share stories, simply and intentionally check in on us to see how we are each doing, make sure we are taking care of ourselves, and let us know they are here. We have received the most thoughtful gifts, books, and cards. It has been, and continues to be, incredibly humbling and heartwarming.

Tomorrow we are due into Cardinal Glennon at 7:15 a.m. for his last scans for surgery prep. A triple-phase MRI and triple-phase CT. We are hoping that the scans continue to validate that the tumor can be successfully removed on February 2. Keep your prayers coming! They are working. We appreciate each one of you.

January 24, 2022

DAY 90.

"For I have plans for you." (Jeremiah 29:11, NRSV-CE)

Hard to believe we have reached the three-month mark. It's been a whirlwind.

Today was Ollie's third MRI and fourth CT scan. It's never easy, as he must be under general anesthesia. But we are so thankful for the amazing staff at Cardinal Glennon and the technology.

Today, the scans, called triple phase with breath holds, were more advanced. This type of scan looks specifically at the veins and arteries and how they interact with his tumor.

To be honest, I had never looked at a picture of a liver prior to this, but there is a lot that runs through that area! How amazing to be able to see to that detail inside.

Ollie did okay with the pre-sedative. They always let me carry him back to the scan room so he can be with me until he is fully asleep.

I'm not going to lie, it's scary. It's overwhelming. Big machines. Lots of medications. Lots of people. Hearing the medical staff do the process-and-procedure rundown. He is so incredibly brave.

Walking out of the imaging area, Brian and I grabbed our pager and headed for coffee. Each morning at Cardinal Glennon, they read a bible verse and say a prayer over the Public Address (PA) System. This ritual is very powerful. Today I immediately recognized the verse, "For I know the plans I have for you," declares the Lord, "plans to prosper you and not to harm you, plans to give you hope and a future." (Jeremiah 29:11, NRSV-CE)

How fitting. Thank you, God, for this message of hope when we were feeling weary.

About two and one-half hours later, our pager rang, and we were able to get down to his room before he woke up. We were home at noon!

His blood work looked great, and he gets to stay off the IVs. He even ate a bit this afternoon.

Our oncologist called and let us know that everything with the scans continues to indicate positive news; tumor shrinking, no spread, and the tumor is moving away from the vascular components of the area.

Thank you, God. Thank you, science.

Thank you, wonderful medical experts, for getting us to this point.

At this point, we will be meeting with the two surgeons over the next week to discuss their approaches to getting his tumor out. Keep praying.

January 31, 2022

DAY 97.

New Surgery Date: Monday, February 7. We have had a wonderful week.

Ollie's energy and mood have been the best they have been throughout this entire ordeal.

It is the first time in twelve weeks he has been off chemo too, so he is most certainly feeling better.

And, we know his tumor has shrunk substantially. Grateful doesn't begin to cover it. We are so incredibly relieved to report that after all the respective disciplines have had the chance to review the 3-D images from last week, consensus still stands that his tumor can be successfully resected, along with part of his liver. His cancer has been extremely responsive to the chemo protocol.

Living in a large metro area, we are very lucky to have many exceptional medical institutions. Since this surgery will be a long, complicated, and high-risk procedure, we were advised to get more than one option on surgical approach, surgical team, and surgical expertise.

We greatly respect and appreciate the professionalism of all the experts we have consulted with. And we are also glad the institutions support each other in doing what is best for the patient.

After speaking with the Children's Hospital Team and the Cardinal Glennon Team; research, advisement, discussions, and prayer; we have for various reasons determined that the Children's Hospital Team and surgical approach is best for Ollie.

It isn't easy for us to leave Cardinal Glennon for this as we have had wonderful care to date, and consistency is important. We just want to ensure that Ollie will have the absolute best chance to be in remission after his tumor is removed.

One technical aspect that differentiated the Children's Hospital Team's approach is using what is called fluorescence guided surgery to help the team. This new technology, in ideal circumstances, in real-time, illuminates cancer cells and helps guide the surgeons to achieve the best margins possible. So, we are moving forward with surgery on Monday, February 7, at Children's Hospital.

A lot of people have been asking how we feel.

On one hand, we are excited and grateful to move forward in this journey. On the other hand, we are terrified for this surgery and his recovery. I am accepting of the dualities the situation has presented to us.

We are all strong and as ready as we can be.

Today's scripture reading at CG was so appreciated too:

"Let not your hearts be troubled. Believe in God; In my Father's house are many rooms. If it were not so, would I have told you that I go to prepare a place for you? And if I go and prepare a place for you, I will come again and will take you to myself, that where I am you may be also. And you know the way to where I am going. Thomas said to him, 'Lord, we do not know where you are going. How can we know the way?' Jesus said to him, 'I am the way, and the truth, and the life.'" (John 14, NRSV-CE)

February 4, 2022

DAY 101. PRE-OP APPOINTMENT AND WORLD CANCER DAY.

Ollie continues to be our amazing, tiny superhero. Today we had his pre-op appointment at Children's Hospital.

He had to have a new IV drawn at a new place, as they couldn't use his existing port. He was so incredibly brave, especially knowing it was going to hurt.

Ollie then got the fluorescent green dye injected, which was interesting, and a COVID swab. We are set for Monday's 5:45 a.m. arrival. Surgery starts at 7:30 a.m. The surgeon said he should be out of surgery by about 2 p.m.

He will then recover in the PICU for a day or two and be transferred for the rest of his recovery to a normal floor once he has stabilized.

Today is World Cancer day. World Cancer day is an international day to raise awareness of cancer and encourage prevention, detection, and treatment.

I dedicate this day in memory of my amazing, strong, brave, and beautiful mother of eight, Colleen, who lost her battle to stage 4, inoperable lung cancer in 1999.

And, I dedicate this day in honor of our tiny superhero, Ollie. Hepatoblastoma survivor who has been fighting cancer since October 2021.

BEHIND-THE-SCENES

I was recently interviewed by *Catholic Saint Louis Magazine* about Ollie's story for the annual Glennon Sunday campaign, sponsored by the Cardinal Glennon Foundation.

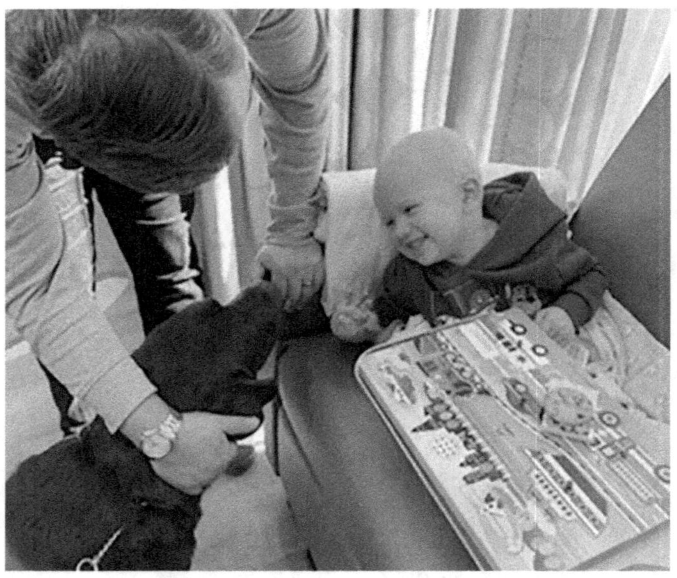

Glennon Sunday is an annual campaign started seventy years ago to raise the seed money needed to build SSM Health Cardinal Glennon Children's Hospital. Cardinal Glennon is the country's first free-standing, non-profit, Catholic pediatric hospital.

The writer asked me, "What was the lesson in this?" Instinctively, I told her, "Always chase the light."

To bring further context to it, I said, "Within years of reflection of the experience I endured at age fifteen with losing my mom, I was now at an age where I was able to lean more directly into my faith with

God. To know that no matter the outcome, good or bad, God would be with us. He would be with me, he would be with Brian, and he would be with Ollie."

February 5, 2022

DAY 102. OLLIE'S BLOOD DRIVE.

Today, the Lakeside Children's Academy, in conjunction with the American Red Cross, hosted a blood drive in Ollie's honor. This drive was held at the Daniel Boone Public Library in Ellisville. This event was meaningful to us and to so many others. I must encourage anyone who can do so to give blood.

The incredible outcome of this blood drive means February 5, 2022, is a day I will never forget! This was a big drive.

RESULTS FROM THE RED CROSS: We ended up seeing fifty-nine presenting donors, twenty-three of which were first-time donors! We collected fifty-nine productive units. These units will help up to 177 patients in need at our partner hospitals.

"Thank you" again to all those who helped and supported the mission of the Red Cross.

CHAPTER 10

SPARKS

Today is theday we have been anxiously awaiting since learning of Ollie's diagnosis on October 25, 2021.

Whew! We knew it would be a long, tough, emotional day. Time to face it head-on.

CaringBridge Chronicles

February 7, 2022

DAY 104. RESECTION DAY!

We arrived at 5:45 a.m. and were called back to our room promptly at 6:10 a.m. A lot happened in eighty minutes to get him ready for his 7:30 a.m. anesthesia time.

We also met with the entire team, including his surgeon, one last time. We were able to carry him all the way back to the double doors, to the sterile surgical area, and the separation wasn't as bad for him as it was for us. He had received a pre-sedative.

Our first update was at 9:30 a.m. At that point he was under general anesthesia; they had run all the IV lines; two in his back, one in each arm. They also used his port, and they had just started the procedure.

At 11 a.m., we got another update that he was stable, doing well. They had just stabilized the liver and were ready to begin the resection.

At 12:30 p.m., they let us know that he was doing well and everything was going as planned.

At 2:00 p.m., they said they were done getting the tumor and the part of his liver out and removing his old scar tissue from his original biopsy. And, one of the surgeons would come soon to speak with us and to let us know how it went.

The sense of relief we had to know he was on his way out of surgery and stable cannot be described adequately.

The surgeon told us that the procedure went exactly as planned. Thank you, God!

The fluorescent injection worked to aid them in guiding for negative margins on what was cancerous and what was not. Those injections also improved their overall level of confidence in what they saw on the scans, further validated through the ultrasound.

They did see some nodules light up that they had tested. Those came back negative, just inflamed tissue. All in all, everything went well.

The pictures the surgical team shared of his liver and cancer are incredible. So glad that his tumor is out!

We were finally able to go back to recovery about 4 p.m. He was waking up, and they were able to get him off his breathing tube! Mildly sedated, he was anxious, confused, and obviously in pain despite the multitude of medications. They cleared a spot for me to lie with him, and we worked to calm him down, which took a while, understandably so.

We were brought up to the PICU around 4:30 p.m. I have been able to lie with him to help him get settled, and with the assistance of some additional pain meds, he is doing okay.

The goal for tonight is pain management and rest.

We continue to lean into receiving the outpouring of strength through our family and friends, lifting us in prayer and thought. Thank you, and keep them coming.

BEHIND-THE-SCENES

Resection day was a day fraught with so many mixed and polarizing emotions. We were absolutely elated that the day was finally here to get the tumor and part of Ollie's liver out. But we were also so scared and anxious about how it would go.

We had been briefed about the high-risk nature of the complex surgery, and honestly, we just held on to hope that the best possible outcome would be produced. Yes, we had been told that death was a possibility and had to sign paperwork acknowledging all this.

Our specific hope was to get the tumor out with adequate margins without complications.

Once we passed Ollie off to the surgeon and his team, we took a big breath. Watching them go through the set of double doors was literally breathtaking. Like the air was sucked out of us. No choice. We had to do it. We had to hold on to hope that it would all be okay. We had to lean into our faith over fear.

The day ahead involved trying to stay calm and to be in prayer. We knew the time would pass slowly. We had to keep ourselves busy. Brian and I walked the miles of indoor walkways for hours. It seemed like it was the only way we could keep our wits about us. We talked a bit and then each listened to music. Music has always been so therapeutic for me. We stopped for coffee and breakfast about 9 a.m. at a cute little café on the indoor walking path between the hospital, Washington University Medical School Buildings, and the parking garages.

Sitting in this moment was hard; it really made my mind race. Thankfully, shortly thereafter, we got the first update call that Ollie was stable, and it was going as planned. I can't tell you how amazing it was to get live updates from the surgical team. After our breakfast, we kept walking. About 1 p.m., we decided that we would go to the Ronald McDonald suite to try to rest our bodies and minds for what was to come.

I found a cozy spot that looked out over the beautiful old trees in Forest Park and wrapped myself in the prayer shawl that Ollie's daycare had given me from Manchester Methodist Church. I gripped a small handheld cross made of olive wood from Jerusalem and looked out the big wall of windows. The sun was bright, and the sky was blue. I tried to just breathe and be.

The leather recliner was comfortable, and I dozed off for a few minutes despite feeling sick to my stomach with worry.

Brian had found himself a quiet, private vestibule with a recliner and a curtain to block out the light. I was glad he was resting too.

We finally got the update about 2 p.m. that the resection was complete, and we would hear from a surgeon soon.

Talking with the surgeons was a bit of a blur, but I do remember they stayed with us and answered all our questions. The green fluorescent dye that was injected worked, and they were able to use the technology to get the best possible margins.

Moreover, all the tissue would also be tested to ensure they achieved the margins they had hoped. All in all, both surgeons were happy with the outcome.

When we did finally get to see Ollie after his surgery, it was such a relief, maybe the biggest relief I have ever felt in my entire life. But I was confused. I thought that he would be intubated for the pain and not really awake. I instinctively thought this because he had been intubated after his biopsy. This surgery was much longer and more complex.

That was not the case, though. I hadn't prepared myself for the state he might be in. I should have known better. I did know better.

The problem was, I was so focused on getting through the surgery that once I saw him, I had an immediate adrenaline rush and then a crash. The doctors explained he was doing great, so they didn't need to keep him intubated and that it would be better for his overall recovery. I did agree, that was awesome. However, the minute we walked in to see him, he was confused, wincing, and crying with pain. He looked so incredibly fragile.

He couldn't cry hard, but he was in a tremendous amount of discomfort and in a foggy state of cognition. This was, of course, to be expected, but so difficult and traumatic to see.

His eyes were closed, and we talked to him, reassuring him we were there with him. It was heartbreaking to see him in that state. Then, the nurses asked me to climb into bed with him. Say what? I was terrified.

Obviously, I wanted to hold my baby, to lie next to him, but I was beyond scared. I had never seen so many tubes connected to a human being in my life.

There were two towers of IVs. He also had a back IV running. It was insane, the number of lines.

The nurses helped me gently onto the bed. I carefully snuggled in. I thought I might throw up from the fear and anxiety of accidentally causing him more pain by sitting on an IV, or worse, causing one to move or come out. He was alive, thank God, but so uncomfortable. There was nothing I could do but try to hold him and verbally reassure him I was there, and he was going to be okay.

My heart broke again. I could feel actual pain in my heart. I wanted to cry.

I had to remain strong, but the intensity of the situation culminated in a major migraine for me. I wasn't entirely surprised. The intense stress, combined with the fact that I also didn't care properly for myself that day, came to a head in my head. That day, I had very little water and had not eaten much.

Thankfully, that night, our aunts, Patti and Marian, brought the most delicious home-cooked meal to the hospital. Brian bravely walked down to meet them, as I didn't want to see or interact with anyone. I distinctly remember going to the family room about 8 or 9 p.m. to eat. I sat in the silence and just stared at the table and tasted the food. I breathed. We had made it through another day. I looked up at the clock. It was late.

I returned to the room after twenty minutes, and I was simply not prepared for what was to come.

The following twenty-four hours would be some of the most difficult and restless in Ollie's entire journey.

February 9, 2022

DAY 106. PROGRESS TOWARDS RECOVERY.

The first night in the PICU was rough. To be expected, but never easy.

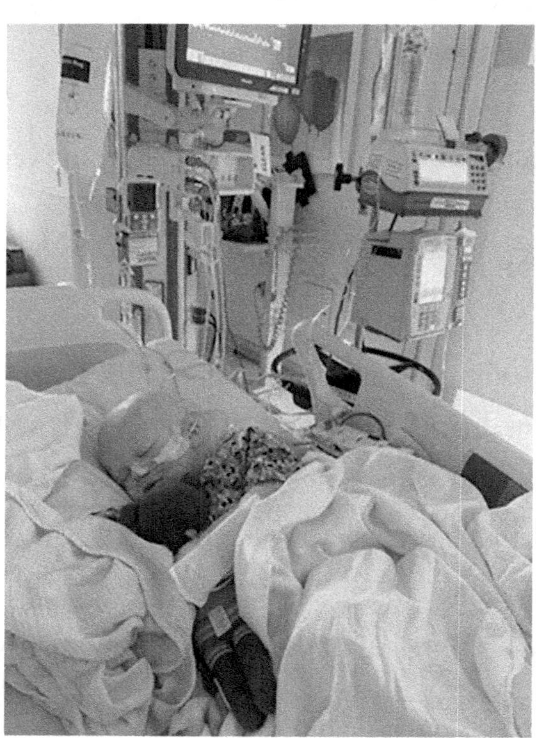

It's tough to rest in the PICU. For anyone.

Extra machines monitoring and beeping, medications to be managed, vitals to be checked.

All the various teams check in frequently; pain management, surgery, and oncology.

Ollie barely slept despite being heavily medicated and sedated.

He started spiking fevers.

He started getting a bit delirious.

We tried absolutely everything to get him to be comfortable and settled, to no avail.

He even had a new therapy dog, Glacier, come and visit.

He was then swabbed for viruses, due to the fevers, then tested positive for adenovirus, with cold-like symptoms.

As the day went on yesterday, we were able to get him off the sedative, which wasn't helping, and he finally fell asleep about 4 p.m. with the help of Valium, a Morphine drip, and Benadryl.

Then, we were moved to the general surgery recovery Floor 10. When we got to Floor 10, we had a special visitor: a mom of one of Ollie's classmates, Emily D., who is an oncology nurse practitioner.

It was so nice to visit with her. Such a small world!

We started to get settled into our new room and suddenly Ollie started having intense interment shakes and his heart rate was spiking. Sensors were going off, with alerts.

He was completely out of it. It was terrifying.

We called the nurses, and the floor doctor also came in.

They did a variety of checks, but ultimately thought it was pain and/or fever-related.

He also had a lot of medication before leaving the PICU that his body was still processing.

Unfortunately, he can't have anything specific for his fevers right now because of his recovering liver. So, we just had to watch, comfort him, pray, and have them pass. These ended by about 8 p.m.

His vitals were monitored very closely overnight.

We are relieved to report that we all were able to get some sleep last night. Brian and I switching halfway through the night as to who got to lie down to sleep and who was stuck in the upright chair.

Ollie was finally somewhat comfortable and only mildly awake, here and there. The nurses were able to remove his IVs off one hand, so now he had one free and wasn't as tethered to the pumps.

He decided to pull out his NG tube from his nose in the middle of the night, but thankfully, that was going to come out today anyways. His catheter also came out this morning. Lots of positive baby steps.

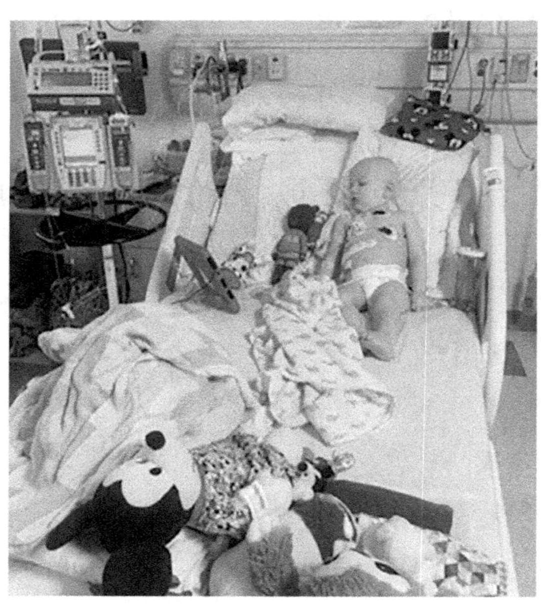

With some help, Ollie has been able to tolerate sitting up and some small sips of water.

His blood tests all looked positive, including the specialized liver tests to analyze enzyme output and processing, and other vitals.

We will work on small steps throughout the day to help him move forward.

We feel encouraged and are grateful for all the amazing medical professionals helping him and for the grace shown to us by God throughout this whole ordeal.

Thank you for your continued prayers, support, and love. We feel them!

February 10, 2022

DAY 107. FIRST STEPS.

Our sweet boy is so incredibly strong.

The days have gotten progressively a bit better. He is fever free and tolerating his breathing treatments, which assist in preventing pneumonia. His Morphine drip got moved to a lower dosage this morning. No Valium needed since Tuesday.

Today, he even took a couple sips of milk and his first few assisted steps to and from the couch.

All his vitals and labs have been stable. Each day we will look to have baby steps towards strength!

Our team is very happy with his overall progress.

Brian and I have found the coffee and some routes for additional indoor walking in the maze of walkways between Barnes/BJC,

Children's Hospital, Siteman Cancer Center, and Washington University Medical School. The connectivity is amazing!

Thank you all for your continued prayers, positive vibes, thoughts, check-ins. We are so grateful for the kindness, love, and support!

February 12, 2022

DAY 109. RECOVERY DAY 5/PATHOLOGY REPORTS.

I sit here, absolutely amazed at our tiny human.

He has been so brave, resilient, and accepting of everything that has happened to him over the past three and one-half months. He is the definition of strong.

Watching him persevere through his diagnosis has been a life journey and a lesson.

Yesterday was a big day. Ollie was able to eat and drink some.

He got up and, with some assistance, walked. We were hoping for just the length of one hallway, but he walked the whole floor! The nurses and doctors are amazed by his strength and determination. The nurses at the station were cheering him on. It was so wonderful. We were incredibly happy and proud of him. A moment I will never forget.

He also came off the Morphine drip, and today, his catheter nerve blocks in his back were removed. We have transitioned to just oral pain meds.

The only tubes he has remaining are his port, which is still providing some fluids, and his drain, assisting with belly fluid. Those will both come off today.

If he can sustain progress with eating, drinking, and managing pain, we "might" be home later today or tomorrow. Absolutely incredible!

This week's journey in and of itself has, in some ways, felt like a lifetime. And, in some ways, now feels like a blink.

Some high highs and low lows. We have continued to stay diligently positive in the present moment. We always work towards focusing on any step forward for our boy, large or small.

This morning, Ollie's surgeon came in with his pathology reports from surgery. A variety of specimens removed during surgery were tested, including peritoneal nodules, diaphragmatic nodules, right hepatectomy/tumor, periportal lymph nodes, skin, and subcutaneous tissue.

We are relieved and excited to report that in all these specimens, there was no evidence of malignant cells.

This is such remarkable news and a huge step forward in Ollie's full recovery. Our hearts feel lighter and our minds more at ease for the first time since October 25.

While we still have two more rounds of chemo (over six total weeks) to complete after Ollie is cleared from surgery, the outcome of the resection was successful and imperative to Ollie's eventual remission.

As we have been walking around the hospital the past few days, there are a lot of signs thanking the healthcare workers for being heroes. I know most of us have seen these signs in the community too; outside hospitals, clinics, and other healthcare facilities, especially since the pandemic started.

It is unfortunate that it has taken this very personal experience for me to have such a refined appreciation for what healthcare workers have chosen to do with their lives and time. Truly important work; saving lives, caring for the most vulnerable and fragile. The work never stops. They are always on.

I will never forget or stop thinking of our heroes. All the various Dr.'s, NPs, Nurses, Technicians, and other Child Life team members who have dedicated themselves to helping people heal, recover, and live.

There are no adequate words for just how appreciative we are. And, to all those who have and continue to lift us in various ways, we wouldn't be here without you either.

So, thank you for your love, support, prayers, friendship, and kindness. Keep praying that the next few months will reveal we are at the end of this journey.

DAY 109 – CONTINUED.

Home Sweet Home!

Not much more to say other than wow! So grateful to be home much sooner than expected thanks to Ollie's incredible resilience and recovery. We are all so happy and will be resting up over the next several days! Thank you, God!

February 18, 2022

DAY 115. SURGICAL FOLLOW-UP – CHEMO CLEARANCE

We have been home for six glorious nights. Ollie has continued to improve rapidly each day!

He climbs stairs, jumps around, and rides his bike. He has been eating and drinking well. It's truly a phenomenal and awe-inspiring sight.

Today we had our follow-up with his surgeon and got the "all clear" to start Round-5 of chemo. It's standard protocol that after you get the Hepatoblastoma out, you follow up with two more rounds of chemo to help ensure all the cancer cells have been eliminated.

This means we will check into Cardinal Glennon on Monday and stay a night or two at 4N. The first days of each new round are the most intense, with Ollie getting several different chemos staggered over time.

While we honestly dread more nights at the hospital, we can now definitely see the light at the end of this dark road we have been on. Six more weeks, if all goes to plan, and then, God willing, Ollie can ring the bell and be in survivor maintenance.

We look forward to enjoying a few weekend days before he gets blasted with chemo again. We are grateful for all the time we have had together through this journey. Staying the path of one day at a time and praying that we continue to remain strong and courageous. Let's finish this!

February 20, 2022

DAY 117. A FULL DAY OF FUN!

A full day of fun was in store for Ollie before we must check back into CG tomorrow for a night, maybe two. The Aquarium, a visit with

Grandma Geen, and a trip to a favorite local park with his new scooter. The weather was incredible for February, and we can really taste spring!

It continues to be remarkable how fast he is recovering from his surgery, which was just two weeks ago, tomorrow. So grateful to see him smiling, laughing, and doing all the normal activities a toddler would enjoy.

Today at the park, which we frequented before his diagnosis, I had to look around. It's almost like this has just been a bad dream, and we will wake up soon.

His laugh on the swing brought me right back to all the fun we nonchalantly had before this. Today really filled my cup.

We are ready to keep moving forward! Six weeks seems so doable. Tomorrow will be a long day, but we know what to expect. Heart tests before labs, then check in, hydration metrics, and then chemo for about twelve hrs.

A family slumber party at Cardinal Glennon; that's what we tell Ollie. Praying and hopeful that the last two rounds of chemo don't cause any permanent damage to his hearing or heart, as that is still a risk, as the chemo is additive. We appreciate your continued thoughts and prayers for Ollie and us!

CHAPTER 11

FIFTH ROUND

February 22, 2022

DAY 119. ROUND-5, DAY 2.

Day 118 was LONG but good.

Ollie got his ECHO screening and EKG first thing at the Cardinal Glennon Dallas Heart Center. Both tests show no damage. We then made our way to the Costas Center at 8:45 a.m. for labs and pre-admit work. We visited with Dr. Lauren, Ollie's oncologist, and she was so happy to see how well he was recovering. Labs all looked good, and so did hydration metrics!

We do have to wait on the AFP number for a day or two, and are anxious to see what that is now.

NP Jenny, the nurse practitioner who helped identify that something was wrong with Ollie's belly the day we took him to urgent care, stopped by! It was so nice to reconnect with her. She also works in the ER at Cardinal Glennon. We hadn't seen her since that day, October 24, and it felt so amazing to be able to give her a hug and talk with her.

Her instinct guided her to have Ollie's case investigated further, as to her, it didn't look like traditional constipation. God truly works in mysterious ways.

She had the x-ray flagged for further review by the radiologists at Cardinal Glennon on that following Monday morning. The expediency to which we were able to get Ollie a diagnosis, October 25, has crossed our minds so many times. Had we had to wait additional days or weeks to find out what was wrong, his thirteen-cm "massive" tumor could have very well grown past intermediate staging and started to encapsulate the IVC or Portal vein. Treatment would have been much more complex.

God led us to NP Jenny after Ollie's fall, and we are so incredibly thankful for her role in helping save Ollie's life. Ollie loved painting the dinosaur nightlight Miss Jenny brought, and building and playing with the cement mixer she gifted him.

NP Jenny is one of our forever heroes. An angel on earth.

Unfortunately, there were some staffing issues yesterday, and we were not able to move up to 4N, the oncology floor, until 2 p.m.

The silver lining was we were greeted by one of our favorite nurses, Miss Kristen! We have had Miss Kristen almost every time we have been admitted since October. She is very special to us and familiar to Ollie. She had his chemo lined up to start about 4:30 p.m.

We also had an awesome visit from art therapist Miss Bri, and she and Ollie played with Play-Doh for an hour, making a pirate scene with piggies and an octopus and pirate treasure chests. Lots of laughter and fun!

Hospital Chaplain Madison also stopped by. She is incredibly calm and thoughtful, praying that we would have a restful night.

Everyone was so happy to see how well Ollie has been doing after his surgery. His energy, strength, and demeanor are so different, so improved these days. You can just see he is feeling better.

The night in general went well. He had his other chemo's administered. About 5 a.m., he got nauseous and sick, but based on past experiences with the Cisplatin chemo, we were halfway expecting that. It certainly doesn't make it easier on him or us, but we were prepared. Our night nurse brought in meds right away, and after about an hour, we had it under control, and we all were sleeping.

I kept thinking to myself as I felt terrible for my sweet baby, only one more dose of this toxic Cisplatin in three weeks.

He woke up happy. Miss Kristen was also back today. He drank milk, had some Cheerios, and a few bites of popsicles.

He has gone on several walks around the floor with "big tubie."

We even saw a little friend who was Ollie's age also out on a walk with his "tubie."

Our favorite resident, Meredith, who has been with us since day 1, also came to say hi! It was wonderful to see her.

Ollie looks so good, all things considered! His last chemo will be administered at 4 p.m., and we should be home by about 5:30! We will administer a shot at home tomorrow, twenty-four hours after chemo, to help his white blood cells regenerate quicker. We have learned how to do that, so we don't have to stay any extra days.

All the thoughts and prayers our tribe continues to send are lifting and sustaining us through this challenge. We feel God with us, telling us that we are almost through this journey.

BEHIND-THE-SCENES

I was asked recently about what made Cardinal Glennon special. What is this "Glennon Factor" people talk about. My response was simply "So many things."

From the moment you walk in, you are greeted by the security team, who are always welcoming, smiling, and often know your name. You smell the fresh coffee and espresso at the coffee kiosk you pass on the way to the atrium. There is a design contest each month for anyone who wants to participate, so every month, the winning, newly designed shirt is on prominent display in the gift shop. The atrium is filled with large-scale climbable models; a train, a double-decker bus, a submarine, and a steamboat. Behind the models are two walls with water bubbles and a large grandfather-type clock that has special features like fairies, a river, and a mouse hole to investigate.

The hallways have beautiful artwork, murals, and more of the whimsical, mystical grandfather-type clocks. Each clock has its own specialized theme, and each is so interesting to the kids when they pass. There is also a large statue of Cardinal Glennon himself.

And, the medical staff is simply amazing. Watching the doctors, nurses, and all the support staff, it is clear by the way they treat each person they encounter, that this is not a job for them, it is truly a calling.

The daily bible verses, broadcast on the PA at 9:00 a.m. sharp, allow you time to pause, pray, and have hope. The housekeeping staff prays over your child each morning when they come in to clean your room. The Child Life staff provides services like art, music, books, and animal therapy. There are TVs on the ceilings in the specialty rooms and many toy closets throughout the facility. The Chaplain visits, and the beautiful chapel space itself is a refuge of calm in the chaos.

The facility just embraces you from the moment you walk in the door. You feel the healing presence of God. It's a physical, mental, emotional, and environmental experience of light and love that I and many others call the "Glennon Factor." It is special. We are so lucky to have experienced it through our darkest of days.

March 1, 2022

DAY 126. ROUND-5, DAY 9.

The sun was shining bright today, and March is finally here!

Ollie spent his morning at Grandma and Grandpa Geen's and came home at noon so we could go to Costas for his outpatient chemo at 1 p.m. He was so happy after his fun morning that it was hard to tell him we had to go to Cardinal Glennon. We mentioned it yesterday to him, so it wouldn't be a complete surprise, to which he told me, "No, Mommy, my belly is all better now."

I wish I could say we were in and out, but these visits typically take about four hours. It's as long as it sounds–especially with a three-year-old in a tiny room. But we make the best of it.

Today, he wanted to have the *Paw Patrol* movie on, play with Play-Doh, construction stickers, eat his Cheez-Its, and build his magnet robots. So, we did a little of all of that!

Brian and I also got our laptops out and did some work in our mobile office. His labs came back, and he was okay to proceed with his chemo for the day. We have to go back on Friday to have his hemoglobin checked again, as he might need another blood transfusion. He also must go back on the at-home overnight IV to help improve his phosphorus and magnesium counts.

We have had a wonderful break from the at-home IV, so we are not thrilled, but we can manage twelve hours. And at this point, I just keep telling myself, "Four weeks of treatment."

We can do it!

Please pray that Ollie's AFP number continues to decline. We did get his update last week, and it is now down to 149 from 850-ish.

This is wonderful progress, but it needs to continue to trend down and get to normal, less than ten.

Our oncologist will be taking this metric weekly for a while. If it goes up, he will need to have scans before the end of treatment.

Tomorrow, we should know the number from today.

Yesterday and today, Ollie received surprise gifts in the mail that really made him feel special! And we had a neighbor friend bring us a delicious dinner last night. We can't say it enough. Thank you all for your continued thoughts, prayers, and kindness to our family. We love you!

March 2, 2022

DAY 127. AFP DECLINE!

Short and sweet post today, thank God. Ollie's doctor just called, and his AFP has dropped by another one hundred. It is now 49! We are trending in the right direction. We were so anxious to hear this news. Now we have some relief.

Keep those prayers coming; we appreciate it more than we could say.

March 4, 2022

DAY 129. LABS.

I am sitting in our living room as I write this, watching our sweet superhero boy dance and sing to Cocomelon.

It seems like a miracle. Literally.

We are just twenty-five days out from when he could barely walk after his major resection surgery.

Ollie's energy, demeanor, and appetite have all been tremendous today. Before the dancing and singing, he sat at our kitchen counter and took bites of what I would characterize as a "meal"; ravioli, Swiss cheese, his favorite, and grapes. All together. This is after eating quite a bit today already!

I can finally breathe deep again. I just stood there and enjoyed him seeming and feeling normal-ish.

We had our lab visit at Costas today to evaluate if Ollie needed a blood transfusion or not. He did not! We were in and out in about three and one-half hours.

Better than eight hours or all day. So, we will take it.

We started the overnight IVs with phosphorus and magnesium again, and Ollie does well accepting little "tubie." He still likes that it's "tubie" who does all the medicine and that he gets to help "tubie" "have a drink."

March 9, 2022

DAY 134. ROUND-5, DAY 17.

Yesterday, Ollie completed the last chemo treatment of Round-5! Fifteen treatments down, three to go.

Labs looked good, and he did not need a blood transfusion. He got his anti-bacterial medicine and his chemo, and we were out by noon.

His magnesium and phosphorus have also stabilized, so he was able to be de-accessed and is off the at-home overnight IVs for now. A little break for him and us. We will get news on his AFP number today.

Prayers that it has continued to decline. Grandma Geen came over for some special one-to-one time in the afternoon so I could make a business trip to and from Cape Girardeau, and so Brian could work. We are so grateful for help! And Ollie absolutely adores his time with Grandma.

We also got fantastic news back from Washington University Genetics that one of two tests we had completed has come back, and Ollie does not have the genetic mutation for APC. Praise the lord! Such a relief.

We will check in again next Tuesday for, hopefully, God willing, our last inpatient chemo. That will be followed by two weeks of outpatient chemo and a set of scans on April 4. If everything looks good,

Ollie will have monthly labs to keep an eye on his overall health, AFP and quarterly scans for the first year. His port can come out after about six months if everything stays clear. Please keep those prayers coming!

March 9, 2022

DAY 134. AFP RETEST.

Well, it's been a day.

Ollie had a fantastic time with his nanny, Miss Kaitlin, who has been so kind to him and to us. It's hard to explain to people just how much their light and love mean.

When she left this afternoon, he wanted to go to the park and the market. Ollie's oncologist called just before 5 p.m. to let me know the results of his AFP lab work from yesterday. It has come back much higher at 900. This is obviously concerning, but she told me that we don't need to worry just yet. She wants to re-test. So, we are going back in tomorrow to have it retested. If it comes back still elevated, he will need to have a set of scans early next week to try to figure out what is going on.

It could also come back as an anomaly. So, we are praying that perhaps there was some error. Results will come back Friday.

We are anxious but know that we can handle whatever is thrown our way. We are so hoping that our journey stays linear and that we are approaching the end.

He has been in such amazing spirits, eating, playing, and being a normal, happy three-year-old who is more like a teenager. We will keep you all posted. Extra prayers, please.

March 11, 2022

DAY 136. MACHINE PROCESSING ERROR.

My God, we have been anxious, confused, and concerned over the past forty-eight hours.

Yesterday morning we went into Cardinal Glennon Costas to repeat Ollie's AFP lab. As we checked in, the daily bible verse and prayer were read at 9 a.m. It was "Be still in the presence of the lord. Wait patiently for him to act." (Psalm 37, NRSV-CE)

I closed my eyes and prayed.

I took a deep breath.

When I opened my eyes, I saw Ollie, smiling, talking, and playing in the atrium with the model submarine "controls."

I thought to myself, *Lord, please let my child be okay. Let him be near the end of this journey. We are tired and weary.*

Once we got back to our room, he was not having it. For the first time, he really gave his nurse a hard time getting his port in. He ripped the first one out, and we had to restrain him on my lap while he was screaming to get it in. That is tough for everyone, especially my boy.

Labs were quick, and they also rechecked his magnesium and phosphorus and levels were still okay! No IVs needed at home. He had to have another COVID swab just in case we needed to come in for scans on Monday, and that is not always a pleasant experience.

Poor sweet boy. Such a trooper!

The music therapist, Miss Kelly, came for a visit, and that made Ollie perk up, playing her new drum and singing songs.

NP Jenny was also at Cardinal Glennon, and we got to see and hug her again. Bless these wonderful people!

We were out about 11:30 a.m., and Ollie was so excited to be able to go to Grandma and Grandpa Geen's in the afternoon! As always, had an absolute blast, especially with bubbles. His special afternoon really made up for his tough morning.

This morning, I am so incredibly relieved, grateful, and ecstatic to report that there was an error with processing the labs from Tuesday.

I am in disbelief.

It turns out that the machine went completely down that day, right after his labs were processed. Ollie's number is fifteen, down from the forty-five last week!

Normal range is less than ten, so we are getting so very close! Praise God! I can't say it loud enough. The relief was simply palpable.

No scans needed Monday. Instead, we will check back in on Tuesday, March 15 for his sixth, and hopefully final, round of chemo treatment. We will likely just have to spend one night, if timing can be achieved. That will be followed by two weeks of outpatient chemo and a final set of scans on April 4. Your prayers and thoughts have meant everything to our family during this most challenging time.

Thank you doesn't seem to suffice, but please know we feel the power and hope of prayer and still need them as Ollie moves closer towards the finish line.

That day that we got the call that his AFP was up was so defeating. In re-reading the CaringBridge entries, I talk often about being relieved. It was like each day represented another mini-milestone.

We had to break it up that way because the big picture was too daunting. So, each time I was able to be relieved, I really, intensely, felt it. It was huge. I also talk a lot about feeling the prayers. How I felt people lifting us in prayer. It was like feeling a sense of calm wash over me. It was by far the most unique and surreal experience of my life, and I felt it throughout Ollie's journey.

CHAPTER 12

SIXTH ROUND

March 15, 2022

DAY 140. ROUND-6, DAY 1.

Round-6! We finally meet.

We have been dreaming of making it to this day. The beginning of what we hope is the end.

It's been a long but good day overall. We checked into the Costas Center at 9 a.m. and were admitted at 4 p.m.

We are so thankful for the little wins today. Ollie is very familiar with Nurse Tori. She is so patient, letting him help her and ask her lots of questions. She is mindful to keep everything moving as fast as she can and even got his Cisplatin started earlier than normal.

Ollie ate great! He is loving Eggo Waffles with peanut butter slathered on top. We brought a bunch from home in a lunch bag so he could have them on demand as we were waiting.

Miss Bri, the wonderful art therapist, visited and brought Ollie to absolute giggles. Watching them is so endearing. We went on lots of "quick walks" with and without "big tubie."

Tonight, once we got checked into 4N, Ollie settled in well, and we have Miss Kristen again as our night nurse! So grateful.

I got to see my sweet fellow Warrior Mom and friend, Sammi. Her son Beckett is four years old and was diagnosed a week before Ollie with Leukemia.

We were across the hall from Beckett's family on our first admit to the hospital, and I'm so grateful God had our paths cross. He just knew I would need Sammi in my life.

I got to do a few laps with her and Beck on 4N. He had his super-cape on and was keeping Sammi on her toes, trying to run with his "tubie."

Please keep them in your prayers; they were discharged tonight after a six-night stay that was supposed to be two.

I also got to meet another Warrior Mom that I was connected with online via a liaison of Friend of Kids with Cancer. Our paths hadn't crossed in person until today and it felt great to meet Laura and give her a huge hug. Her son Zion, who is seventeen, has recently relapsed out of remission from T-cell Leukemia and is in desperate need of a match for a bone marrow transplant. Today they were told that their girls, ages fourteen and eleven, are not a match for Zion's bone marrow.

They need a match elsewhere. They are told there are currently three "ten out of ten matches" for Zion globally. This is where we need your help!

To get swabbed to see if you are a match, please go to bethematch. org. You can sign up to have a kit mailed to you. They will put your information into the registry, and if you match for Zion, it will alert their coordinator. There is no need to put his name in. Even if you are not a match for Zion, your bone marrow may be the answer to another person's prayer.

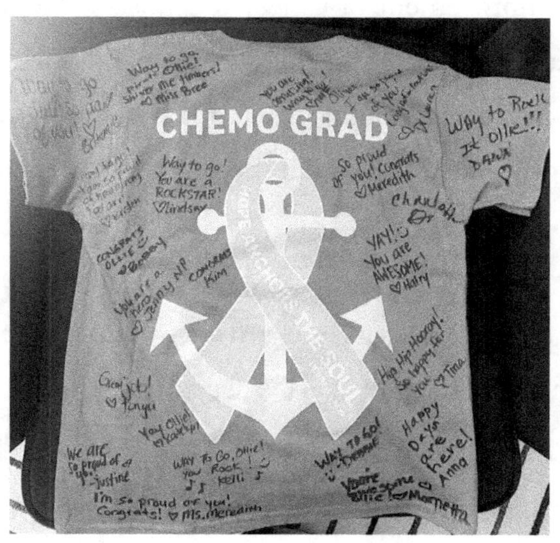

Please consider signing up. It would mean the world to these families. I gave Laura a huge hug, and my heart was so heavy leaving her as we walked to our respective hallways on 4N. Her journey has started over, and they are on night thirteen of this most recent admit. They are on day 875 in their journey.

Being here, on Ollie's journey, and also learning about and seeing other journeys has really impacted me. You simply can't look at life the same after going through something like this.

You're not the same person.

It's equally heartbreaking and inspiring each time you are here to see the kids, parents, and families affected by this disease. There are so many!

And I know I've said it before, but I can't understate it. Those of you who, as medical professionals, have dedicated your lives to the study of and improvement of cancer diagnosis, genetics, treatment, and general care for these kids, "You Are Amazing."

We will be forever grateful to Cardinal Glennon and Children's Hospital. I hope to find meaningful ways to help support these organizations moving forward.

Hopefully, Ollie will have a decent night. He does usually get nauseous and sick after this chemo, but we will do our best to have the nurses stay on top of the anti-nausea drugs.

He is sleeping soundly now, so we will try to sleep too. Thank you for your continued prayers for Ollie and all his friends here. We love you all.

March 17, 2022

DAY 142. AFP CONFIRMATION.

I didn't write yesterday because I wanted the updated AFP number, and it didn't come back until today, but good news, it confirmed our second reading-retest from last week. Ollie's AFP is at 13.9! This is extremely positive and reassuring. Thank you, God. We will get another reading on this number again as part of his labs on his last treatment day, March 29.

The finish line is becoming less blurry. Each day we are moving one step towards it.

We were discharged from Cardinal Glennon yesterday, about 5:30 p.m., after Ollie got his final chemo for day 2 of Round-6.

He did so well through the night. He was only mildly nauseous and thankfully controlled with the use of a third anti-nausea med.

He was up early, and we walked laps around 4N for a good hour with "big tubie." Ollie even went for a wagon ride and then spent time playing in the playroom.

All the nurses were commenting on how much better he looked and seemed to feel. We agreed. His energy was like nothing we have yet seen at the hospital.

We are so incredibly proud of him for his ability to adapt and accept this situation with relative ease, all things considered, and to be brave when he is scared. He is an amazing fighter who will overcome this and be stronger for it.

Today he got to spend special time with his nanny, Miss Kaitlin, and is now at Grandma and Grandpa's. We continue to be so grateful to all the helpers of this world. Whether in person, in spirit, or in thought, your help in various ways continues to get us through. Two more weeks. Keep those prayers coming!

March 22, 2022

DAY 147. ROUND-6, DAY 7. TREATMENT NO. 17.

"Let us run with endurance the race that was set before us." (Hebrews 12: 1, NRSV-CE) This bible verse has been another of my longtime favorites and is very fitting for many stages of life, especially trials and tribulations. When I've felt overwhelmed and needing realignment, focus, and strength, this quote has helped.

At the start of this journey, I knew we were about to start a marathon.

There were so many unknowns, and it was terrifying, physically, mentally, and emotionally. I knew it would be exhausting and traumatic.

To be there for our son and help him through this, Brian and I would have to work hard to stay positive and hopeful despite our tremendous fear and despair.

My sweet colleague, who is now a five-year survivor—shoutout to Becky K. on this milestone—gave me the most beautiful card recently with a quote about endurance.

"Endurance: To stand one's ground; persevere; remain steadfast; courageous; one who does not lose hope in the face of obstacles, persecutions, or trials."

I thought to myself, *we have endured, especially our sweet warrior Ollie, and I am so incredibly proud.* Today was his seventeenth (17th!) chemo treatment.

Whew. He is basically a professional at this now.

What a long, strange trip we have all been on.

Our appointment went smoothly, thanks to Nurse Tori. Ollie's labs looked stable, so he did not need a blood transfusion, to stay accessed, or to come home on fluids.

No AFP reading this week. That next reading will be on March 29 and then monthly thereafter. He got his chemo, and we were out by 12:30 p.m. He passed the time today munching on baked BBQ chips and multi-grain Cheerios, watching his pirate shows. He is at Grandma and Grandpa Geen's this afternoon for his special time.

Ollie will ring the bell next Tuesday at noon outside Cardinal Glennon.

Hurray! We are truly almost to the finish line. It will be an emotional and happy day.

Ollie is overwhelmed by crowds, so we will keep this a smaller group. I'll message you information! And, I will have someone record the ceremony to share with others.

We can't wait to hear the sound of that bell! Thank you all for helping us endure this race. We absolutely could not have done it without your loving and generous support, compassion, positive affirmations, and prayers for each of us.

It takes a village. God is good!

BEHIND-THE-SCENES

Since this experience, I have thought a lot about the "village" I speak of here. We were so lucky to have one. We had employers who were flexible with us, we had good health insurance, Health Savings Accounts (HSAs), and money to pay for the many out-of-pocket expenses. We had grandparents nearby, brothers, sisters, aunts, uncles, cousins, friends that were like family, colleagues, neighbors, professional acquaintances, and many others that showed up for us.

We had it all, and many who rallied for us. They helped us in so many different ways we didn't even know we needed.

So that leads me to the question: What about the people who do not have a tribe, or a job, or health insurance? How do they make it through?

That is a large part of my "why" in being called to give back to Cardinal Glennon.

Please take a moment to read about Cardinal Glennon's Mission in the final pages of the book, along with my personal commitment to the organization. My "why" is personal. My "why" is emotional and physical. It is with my whole being that I believe in the power of miracles. And they happen every day at that facility. It took my personal experience to feel that way, yet Cardinal Glennon was there for Ollie whether he needed it or not. It will be there for all the others who need it too. It's an amazing, impactful community institution.

March 29, 2022

DAY 154. ROUND-6, DAY 15. TREATMENT NO. 18.

"Hope anchors the soul." (Hebrews: 6:19, NRSV-CE) It's truly difficult to adequately articulate the intense feelings of gratitude in a situation that still feels somehow surreal.

Overwhelming appreciation in a way that is more than anything you have ever felt before. How do you express to the people and institutions a thank you for literally saving your child and giving you hope?

Today is the day. Bell ringing day. We made it. After Ollie was administered his eighteenth (18th!) chemo treatment.

Tears streamed down my face as we see our tribe cheering, with bubbles, noise makers, posters.

Just wow. The people who have been there through it all. On the good days, the bad days, and all the days in between. For your prayers, love, support, comfort, and help in any way you could, "Thank you!"

It was a full-circle life experience that has been condensed into five months and culminating today by Ollie ringing that BELL.

NP Jenny was there, our hero who helped identify at urgent care that something wasn't right, and no doubt helped get Ollie to a quicker diagnosis.

Resident Meredith, who was part of the medical team that had to collectively come into the ER room that awful day to tell us our child had cancer. She comforted me in my shock and despair. She held my hand and told me it would be okay. And, she has made a distinct effort to come check in on us throughout this ordeal, visiting us numerous times at Cardinal Glennon.

Nurse Kristen, who was also there with us throughout all our stays; from the very beginning to the very end. Who was one of our night chemo warriors, working tirelessly to bring as much comfort to Ollie and us as she could, throughout our many stays in the hospital. She also consoled me as I fought back tears as Ollie got his head shaved, and he was losing all his hair.

The numerous Child Life specialists, Ms. Bri and Ms. Kelly, the art and music therapists, have been absolute godsends. Their gift is truly incredible. They give these kids moments of normalcy amidst the awful reality of their diagnosis and treatment. For all the hours you brought joy and calm to Ollie, and to Brian and me, "Thank you!"

You are special beyond words.

To our Lakeside Children's Academy Family; Mrs. Sue, Mrs. Laura, Mrs. Annie, Mrs. Di, and all those joining in spirit; you all have been there from the very beginning.

From the day I had to call Mrs. Laura to let her know what happened, and throughout all of this. Showing up for us constantly. Arranging very special days like the Salvation Army Band/Carolers with Mrs. Di, Santa's Visit at our House, the Red Cross Blood Drive on February 5, 2022, in Ollie's honor, sponsoring our family and Cardinal Glennon for Christmas, and all the special notes, posters, and messages. Your kindness and compassion are beyond words.

Jordan, Katie, and baby Jackson, we are so grateful for your love, support, and friendship!

Aunt Michelle, we were so glad you could come too! Your love, prayers, and hopefulness have been steadfast.

Our sweet nanny, Miss Kaitlin, who went above and beyond for Ollie and our family. Your patience and kindness are amazing. You have helped support and lift us with light through the absolute worst times we could imagine. Your strength and grace were sent from God.

And Mom and Dad Geen, two of the most selfless, steadfast, kind, smart, and faithful people you could ever meet. We absolutely could not have made it through this without your constant love, support, and help with caring for Ollie.

Dr. Lauren, Ollie's oncologist hero, we were beyond blessed to be able to work with you. Your knowledge, patience, compassion, and communication are exemplary. We have felt constantly reassured that there was always a plan and a path forward for Ollie, even if it wasn't as straight as we initially hoped. You always gave us all the information and choices and worked tirelessly to ensure the best options were being provided to him. We could never thank you enough.

Today was about celebrating what we set out to do.

Completing the chemo protocol for intermediate risk Hepatoblastoma. It was a long journey, but we never lost hope thanks to our faith in God, our wonderful tribe, and all of you.

Monday, April 4, he has his end-of-treatment scans and will also be administered a hearing and heart test for his new baseline.

We continue to hope and pray that this is the end of cancer for our brave warrior, Ollie. We will get his AFP reading from today, tomorrow. That will be indicative of where his body is, and we are hoping for that number to continually drop to less than 8.

If Ollie's scans are clean next week, he will be declared in "remission." Monthly AFP readings and quarterly scans for the first year will occur. Ten to fifteen percent of kids with Hepatoblastoma have recurrences in the first five years, so keep Ollie in your prayers. He still has a way to go in his recovery. Also, because there is not enough data on pediatric cancer and long-term side effects from the various chemos, his heart, especially, will be monitored for early coronary artery disease.

I say all this, but I am also shouting that we are thrilled to be at what we hope is the end. We need to stay vigilant. We also would still appreciate your thoughts and prayers as we progress through his, and our, recovery.

His special shirt from his care team said it best

"HOPE ANCHORS THE SOUL!"

CHAPTER 13

THE AWAKENING

April 4, 2022

DAY 160. RELIEF. GRATITUDE PRAISE.

It's the day we have been waiting for. Both patiently and impatiently.

160 days since our lives were unexpectedly turned upside down and shaken.

You could likely tell in my last post the absolute happiness of ringing the bell, but also the true anxiety and apprehension about what was next.

We had to make it through today to be shown the results of Ollie's treatment protocol.

It was a long day for our sweet boy.

It started with fasting. Try explaining the concept to a three-year-old. Our appointment was at 10:30 a.m. at Cardinal Glennon for labs and some scheduled medicine. His favorite, Ms. Bri, the amazing art therapist, came by for over an hour and brought fun art supplies for Ollie to create a piece for the upcoming *Friends of Kids with Cancer Art Show*.

He did SO well until about 12:30 p.m. when he had a straight-on panic attack, so upset that he couldn't eat. Tired of sitting in a small room. Didn't understand why we were withholding food from him. Started hyperventilating. It is the worst we have seen him throughout this whole ordeal. Ollie plain just had enough.

Unfortunately, we were not yet done for the day, we headed down the hall at 1:30 p.m. for his procedural anesthesia for his CT scan, audiology test, and ECHO screening. Ollie was so worked up that when we got to the CT area, he thankfully fell asleep really quickly, after, of course, pleading for Cheerios and spicy chips.

He was still shaken, hyperventilating in his sleep for a good twenty minutes. Thank God he stayed asleep until they started the sedation, and that was helpful, as usual, to get him back to the room with the scanning machines.

I was able to carry him back as I always do, and Child Life Services was in there with some distracting toys.

It's an overwhelming environment, no matter how many times you have done it, and I'm so glad I can stay with him until he is fully sleeping.

Brian and I then went up to the Ronald McDonald House to wait, and were so happy to rest in the comfy recliners.

Two hours later, we were back down in recovery as Ollie was waking up. We had an amazing nurse who treated us with such care.

Our oncologist called ten minutes after we got to recovery and let me know to call her back to discuss the scans. I was absolutely panicked.

I didn't expect to hear from her so soon. She had said she would talk with us tomorrow. But what she shared was, she "Didn't want us to wait to hear." Ollie's scans came back perfectly clear!

Stunned.

Relief.

I felt myself let the full-on tears come. I said out loud, "I feel like I can breathe again." Truly! What incredible news.

The words we have been waiting to hear since diagnosis day.

When we got off the phone with Dr. Lauren, Brian and I gave each other the biggest hug.

Our prayers, our faith, our hope, our love, our caregivers; the many doctors and nurses, science, technology, and all the long days and nights endured since October 25. We were here. The finish line.

We made it.

To be able to look at my child in that recovery bed as he was still sleeping; to think and dream for a few minutes of what life would be like again after this nightmare, was the most incredible and happy feeling. Praise be to God for this gift.

The gift of life.

Tonight, when we got home around 5:30 p.m., Ollie was in the best mood. He was singing and jumping on his trampoline, and we built his marble track.

It was, as one of my dear friends said, like it was all a bad dream. His resilience is hard to describe, as it is truly mind-blowing.

Ollie, we can't wait to see what God has in store for you.

We will get his updated AFP reading tomorrow. We would expect this to be congruent with the images and be dropping.

If that blood indicator shows stability or a drop, we will likely be able to transition to once-monthly labs.

We are so ready for what is next. We are ready to have our lives back, individually with Ollie included, but also collectively as a family.

It's been the hardest journey to endure.

We could not have done it without the outpouring of prayers, hope, love, and strength we were given from you all, physically, mentally, and emotionally. I will say it for the rest of my life, "Thank you." We will be forever returning the grace given to us in any way we can.

May 4, 2022

DAY 190.

Yesterday we went back to Cardinal Glennon for Ollie's first follow-up labs, the most important being the AFP number.

He did so well with getting his port re-accessed, and we loved seeing and hugging all the familiar faces in the Costas Center. It's such a close group of humans that truly feels like family to us.

We spoke with Dr. Lauren about the statistics, different scenarios should the AFP come back different than we had hoped, and continued to pray, hope, and have faith that the worst of this is behind us.

But to be honest, until we get the results, it's difficult for the thought not to consume us. Ollie's favorite art therapist, Miss Bri, came and spent time with him, asking him about the special pirate art he made for the upcoming art show that benefits Friends of Kids with Cancer.

Their laughter filled my heart.

Today we learned that Ollie's AFP came back at 6.2!

Relief, joy, happiness. It's hard to adequately explain, but we are so overwhelmed with gratitude for this positive, uplifting news! Normal is less than 10. So, we have made it. This is his new baseline.

We are due back in one month for repeat labs and his first set of scans since April. Keep praying God's grace and love is amazing.

May 18, 2022

SEASIDE SWEETNESS

A happy, elated post that we are enjoying a much-needed family vacation, with my amazing in-laws, in Santa Rosa Beach, Florida. We booked this trip at the end of March after Ollie's oncologist said, "Yes! Do it!" Oliver is having the time of his life, and so are we, seeing our sweet warrior boy be a child again.

Thank you to everyone for your continued thoughts and prayers. We are so grateful for them, for all of you, and for these moments we can spend together.

June 1, 2022

DAY 217.

Back to School! Yesterday, after seven months away, Ollie returned to Lakeside Children's Academy. Happiness and disbelief, we had come full circle. We have, God willing, made it through the worst.

Ollie has attended Lakeside since he was twelve weeks old, so he really missed his teachers, his friends, and the routine/space he was accustomed to! I should also mention he really missed Mrs. Judy's food! He couldn't wait to go back.

The love we felt during this whole ordeal from our Lakeside family will be something we never forget.

They showed up for us in ways I could have never imagined; special posters, cards, gifts, phone calls, messages of concern, love, support, a private at-home Santa Visit, Christmas Sponsorship, and the Blood Drive on February 5.

Just wow!

It says so much about the character of people when they show up for you at your worst and hold your hand through the marathon nightmare. Mrs. Laura, the Academy's Owner/Director, was one of the very first people I called when we found out Ollie's diagnosis, and we cried in disbelief together.

Yesterday, it felt almost surreal to hug her and have her welcome us back. Ollie was so incredibly happy when he came home. He had his art, a dinosaur egg, and was singing and dancing. That joy we feel is indescribable after the last seven months!

And to our special nanny, Miss Kaitlin. We are eternally grateful for you. For helping us day after day and being brave, strong, kind, and patient to stick with a strong-willed three going on thirteen-year-old. "You Are Amazing."

Monday, June 6, we are due at Cardinal Glennon first thing for his CT scan and labs. Continue prayers for positive results and continued remission.

June 7, 2022

DAY 223 — CT, AFP, AND COVID

I know many of you reached out yesterday asking about Ollie's first scans since he ended treatment in March. We were lucky to be very first on the schedule and in and out by 9:30 a.m.

Ollie did great with the sedation, and his overall anxiety was low. Amazing considering we haven't been to Cardinal Glennon in a while. He is such a trooper.

All his labs and his CT looked great yesterday. No changes from the last scan, which is exactly what the doctors are looking for. We are incredibly relieved and grateful to clear another hurdle.

Unfortunately, we ended the day with a trip to the ER. Ollie spiked a high fever late yesterday afternoon, and they wanted him to come in immediately to see what was going on. Code sepsis was called, which meant they had one hour to get labs drawn, swabs, antibiotics started, and results.

The good news is that his body was very responsive to the fever reducer. We can't give at home until they verify he doesn't have a bloodstream infection.

He started feeling better within two hours. Bad news is he has COVID. We have avoided it as a family for twenty-six months, but it finally caught us. Because he is still considered immunocompromised, the ER doctors consulted with the on-call oncologist, and they considered having him stay for monitoring and to start Remdesivir, which would require a three-day admission.

Because he was acting his normal self and singing and climbing and overall happy, we asked if we could monitor his condition overnight at home and re-evaluate in the morning with his doctor. They agreed that would be okay.

He had a normal night. No additional meds needed, no fever. He woke up happy, eating, drinking, and thankfully, no symptoms. He has continued all day to be okay! We spoke with his oncologist, and she was not overly concerned based on how he is doing.

Keep your prayers coming that he just continues to have mild symptoms.

Most importantly, his AFP we found out today is 3.3! This is the most incredible news and indicative of what we see in terms of his overall recovery.

He has continued to improve each day. He is his old, happy, silly, and funny self, enjoying life and feeling good! If his COVID stays mild, we just have to go back next month for labs.

One step closer each month out.

Thank you all for your continued thoughts, prayers, and support.

June 27, 2022

DAY 242: CARDINAL'S PATIENT OF THE GAME

We were able to experience a most memorable day at Busch Stadium with Ollie being recognized as SSM Cardinal Glennon Patient of the Game! We got to go out on the field, share a few bits of our story, and talk about why Cardinal Glennon is so important to us and our community on the Jumbotron. Then Ollie got to throw a first pitch and to meet Fred Bird!

What a full circle day for our family. We are so proud of Ollie and the work Cardinal Glennon does day in and day out saving lives.

We enjoyed the game right below the homers for health sign and my in-laws Jerry and Anna got to update the homers board three times!

Ollie would have loved to help, but he was busy exploring and having fun at the family pavilion and jungle gym.

It was a day we will never forget. Thank you to the Cardinals and Cardinal Glennon for the experience.

June 30, 2022

DAY 245: GIVING BACK, INCREASING CHILDHOOD CANCER AWARENESS.

I often think about how very important it was in our journey that we had access to the Cardinal Glennon facilities specializing in Children's Care.

The new urgent care facility in South County is only a mile or two from our house. The hospital is less than ten miles.

The day we were called to come to the ER immediately after visiting the urgent care the evening before, will be a day we will never forget. I will also never forget the professionals, the technology, the processes, the care, the intention, the compassion, and empathy that were shown to us by all the staff.

The ability to have a diagnosis and treatment plan within forty-eight hours was unreal and absolutely lifesaving for Ollie .

Each year, the Cardinal Glennon Foundation has several fundraisers. One of these is called the *Sun Run*. Ollie and I ran this together in 2018 when I was pregnant with him! Running has been an important part of my life for many years for both physical and mental health, so this event is a great fit for us. Talk about full circle. Ollie will now be one of the children recognized at this event.

The fundraiser will be Sunday, October 16, 2022, at Forest Park in Saint Louis, Upper Muny Parking Lot: 9 a.m. start, 5K Run or one-mile walk. Join and/or donate to: Ollie's Trane!

July 18, 2022

DAY 263: AFP REPEAT

I didn't post two weeks ago when we got the results of Ollie's AFP. But when Dr. Lauren called and didn't text, my heart sank a bit.

The number has risen, just by three points, to 6, and she wants him to repeat the test tomorrow, July 19. We are hoping and praying that the number stays the same and has not increased again.

Any AFP number 10 or under is considered "normal," so we are still within range.

However, this is the number they will watch closely to identify if his body isn't recognizing cancer cells. The AFP is the blood marker to determining if Ollie stays in remission. Keep those prayers coming.

July 20, 2022

DAY 265: ABSOLUTE RELIEF!

Dr. Lauren called early to let me know his number came back at 3.6! We will take that! Absolutely fantastic news. Now we can breathe deep again, and Ollie can continue to thrive. Thank you all for your unwavering care, concern, love, and prayers. It means everything! We will go back for his regularly scheduled monthly test in early August. While these tests are stress and anxiety-inducing, they are critical checkpoints in his recovery and remission.

August 9, 2022

DAY 284 – MONTHLY AFP – GOOD NEWS

Last week, Ollie had his monthly AFP reading. I am so relieved and happy to report it came back at 4! We have been busy enjoying summer with family, friends, and colleagues.

Ollie loves being back at Lakeside Children's Academy.

We are working on our "new normal". I'd still say "recalibrating" from this ordeal.

Two amazing upcoming events we are fortunate to promote and be a part of to support the institutions that helped our family and so many others.

September 24 and 25, 2022, in St. Louis, will be *Pedal the Cause*, St. Louis Children's Hospital. Brian's employer, Enterprise Bank & Trust, has graciously put together a team for this event, and Ollie is the honoree and team captain! Brian is riding Saturday, and I'm riding Sunday. Join us!

The Cardinal Glennon *Sun Run*, which my employer, Trane, has coordinated a team for a 5k (three miles) or a one-mile walk. We would love to have you join us on Sunday, October 16, 2022, at 9 a.m. in Forest Park in St. Louis.

Our next appointment is September 12 for a CT scan and AFP draw. Hoping to get his port out shortly thereafter!

September 13, 2022

DAY 319. DAY OF JOY AND RELIEF.

Almost disbelief that we have come so far. I was talking with some colleagues today, as I am at a team event in Kansas City, and everyone has been so kind to ask about Ollie. I stop and think for a minute.

It's been a race.

It's been exhausting.

This ordeal has really felt like what I would characterize as an ultra-marathon. But a marathon, even the ultramarathon, has an ending. And the ending is always the best part.

Ollie had his 6-month scans and blood test on Monday, September 12, and I feel overwhelmed with gratitude to say that his scan came back perfect, and his AFP is 3!

This means he can get his central line/port out. Praise God.

He is scheduled for September 28 for this surgery, almost eleven months to the day he got it in.

The protocol moving forward is a blood test and ultrasound quarterly, so we are entering a whole new book. Less frequent appointments and no remaining gear in his little body. No medications either!

Thank you all for your continued thoughts and prayers for Ollie and our family.

We are a different unit than we were before this happened.

Stronger.

Completely resilient.

Grateful for every day and living life as full as we can. I think that is the forever lesson in all this.

September 22, 2022

DAY 328. WE CELEBRATE.

The first of many upcoming survivor celebrations!

Tonight was the much-anticipated *Art from the Heart* event sponsored by Friends of Kids with Cancer.

Wow! The event blew us away.

Friends of Kids' mission: helping kids with cancer be kids! Friends of Kids is devoted to enriching the daily lives of children undergoing treatment for, and survivors of, cancer and blood-related diseases. Their mission is to be an advocate for these special kids, providing them and their families with the educational, emotional, and recreational support needed because of the long hours of chemo, illness, and isolation.

We got to see some very special people tonight, Dr. Lauren, Ollie's oncologist, and Miss Bri, our favorite art therapist, who spent countless hours with our family both inpatient on 4N and outpatient in Costas Center.

Ms. Bri helped Ollie feel like a kid with fun art like play-dough, painting, stampers, scissors, and many other art projects. Many days Ollie's mood would instantly improve when he saw his special Miss B.

The music therapy program is also funded through this amazing organization. Social workers visit you when you are first admitted and dealing with this life-shattering news. Aleeza and others were always checking in on us to see how we as parents were holding up.

They deliver resources, meals, snacks, and hugs.

What they do truly makes you feel seen and cared for as care-givers. It's a big part of that distinguishing "Glennon Factor" I have talked about.

Tonight, Ollie's art entitled "*Waves*" was featured as part of the silent auction. Ollie worked on this piece with Miss Bri over several visits to Cardinal Glennon and depicts his love for pirates, treasure maps, and the ocean.

We also got to see Beckett's family, who, like us, had just been admitted to 4N a few days before Ollie last year. They were our neighbors for the first ten days we stayed in-patient at the hospital. To see Beck and Ollie standing outside Cardinal Glennon with no "tubies" on, and not in distress from being poked or prodded, was so heart-warming and surreal.

What a year it has been.

Beckett is still undergoing treatment for his Leukemia and will do so until February 2024.

These kids are the definition of strength and resilience.

Tomorrow is *Pedal the Cause* with Team Enterprise Bank. Team Captain Ollie Geen! Brian is riding twenty-eight miles on Saturday, and I'm riding twenty-eight miles on Sunday.

Tomorrow we will attend the VIP event with Ollie.

September 28, 2022

DAY 334. PORT OUT!

And just like that, eleven months after insertion, his port is out. A huge exhale from us. Ollie did great with the outpatient surgery, which was quick. We were in and out in about two and one-half hours, and conducted by the same surgeon who initially put his port in last October.

Cardinal Glennon staff were all amazing as usual. Keeping the kids' comfort and contentment first. To be honest, today was another incredible relief and also a bit surreal.

It's still unbelievable that this was our reality this past year. I could have never in a million years predicted this as part of my life story.

Ollie was able to rest most of the afternoon. When he woke up, he ate, drank, and enjoyed playing and lounging. Our precious boy. He didn't complain once.

He is an ultimate warrior of strength and perseverance.

We also wanted to say that the *Pedal the Cause* event hosted last weekend was a wonderful and moving event. We appreciate more than we could say Enterprise Bank and Trust for sponsoring the event and a team, which they have done for years, and for naming Ollie the honorary captain this year.

What a memorable and personal experience for us. Once in a lifetime! And thank you to many of you for your generosity in supporting us and our team. It takes a village and ours is strong.

October 16, 2022

DAY 352. CARDINAL GLENNON *SUN RUN* CELEBRATION!

A day to celebrate Ollie and all the kids, past and present, of Cardinal Glennon.

Our hearts were beaming to have so many of our loved ones at one place for this amazing cause.

To feel our community of support, to be able to give hugs and smile, was just amazing.

Ollie was one of the children recognized at this event, and our Ollie's Trane Team was the largest team in the *Sun Run* history with 160 plus members.

We also raised $15,282, coming in second out of seventy-two teams.

I'm so proud of our team and grateful to give back to this special place.

We are approaching the one-year anniversary of Ollie's diagnosis, and to be able to be where we are at today makes me eternally thankful to God and all those involved in healing him and supporting us.

His next appointment isn't until December, and we are welcoming the change in frequency of doctors' appointments.

Ollie's oncologist, Dr. Lauren, NP Jenny F., Nurse Kristen, Nurse Maddy, Nurse Tori, Ollie's nanny Miss K, and Grandma and Grandpa were all our VIP special guests today, as they were our core treatment team and support through this ordeal. We love you all and will never forget this experience.

December 15, 2022

DAY 418

Tuesday, December 13, was our regular scheduled checkup at Cardinal Glennon. The first since the end of September!

This has been the longest duration between appointments since Ollie's diagnosis. Instead of a CT scan this time, he just had to do an ultrasound and an x-ray.

Hooray for no sedation and no anesthesia again. Huge difference in how involved the procedures are and how Ollie feels before, during, and after.

The ultrasound took about twenty minutes, followed by labs, x-ray, and then his Costas Center appointment. Since this was the first time doing labs without his port, Brian and I were a bit anxious, but Ollie did amazing! He is such a strong and easy-going boy, especially considering all he has been through. We continue to be so proud of him. The ultrasound and x-ray came back perfect, and his labs/AFP are great. Still at 3.5! Such wonderful and hopeful news to continue to build on his recovery.

I told Brian that each month we get further out from his bell ringing, the less anxious I feel. While we know the cancer can still come back, the probability of it decreases with time.

Next appointment will be at the end of March for his one-year CT and labs. We sincerely appreciate everyone who has and continues to think of and pray for us.

We were also asked to help the Cardinal Glennon Foundation with a special project, and Ollie and I spent most of the day Tuesday helping with that. It was incredibly interesting and fun, and we are glad to be able to give back.

Ollie has also been asked to be a Children's Miracle Network Ambassador for 2023.

We look forward to connecting with other families and the community to bring awareness and raise funds for our phenomenal local institutions that save lives!

Happy Holidays and New Year to you all. By the grace of God, we couldn't be more relieved, happy, and grateful to be where we are today.

January 10, 2023

DAY 444. WISH KID

When the Make-A-Wish team first called me in November 2021, we were three or so weeks into Ollie's diagnosis. I'll never forget the call.

It was a warm fall afternoon, and we were in the car driving to Watson Trail Park in Sunset Hills to get some nature time, fresh air, and play. Outside activities were mostly all of what we could do, and we both needed to get out. I answered on speaker phone, and they asked if it was a good time to talk.

I remember being a bit stunned when they said who they were with.

They explained that Ollie qualified for a wish and that the local Chapter would be reaching out soon.

I remember thinking, "Do they know something I don't about Ollie's diagnosis? Was he not going to make it?"

Make-A-Wish, in my mind, was only for kids with terminal illnesses. My mind raced through the images of Wish Kids I've seen or heard of in the past, ones that were recognized in public places or on TV ads, like at sports games. Most of these recollections were difficult to think of, in the sense that the kids were typically bald, ill, and generally not well.

I answered the ladies' questions, trying my best to hold it together, but also a bit panicked and overwhelmed. Never in a million years would I have thought that my kid would be a Wish Kid.

Never would I have thought he'd have cancer at the precious age of two, and be offered a wish through this tremendous international organization.

I was trying to process it all. The diagnosis, our current life, our future life, what it all meant, and how it was going to be.

We met our wish granters, Wendy and Molly, via Zoom sometime in December 2021. Ollie was being cute, marching all over the house, bald, in his diaper, and playing his pretend trumpet.

He wouldn't sit much for the Zoom call, but that was okay. Wendy and Molly just asked us to share a bit about him, his likes, interests, and his personality.

In the spring of 2022, Molly and Wendy came over for a meet and greet and brought sticky notes to write down the details of what Ollie was sharing. Really just words, lots about Mickey Mouse and animals. The exercise was to meet Ollie where he was at and learn more about him.

Wendy and Molly came up with several ideas that we presented to Ollie, and he picked to meet Mickey Mouse and see the "castle."

A lot of planning goes into these wishes, and the granters are the most patient, kind, and big-hearted people, some who have had their own kids granted wishes, too.

We have been actively coordinating the details of this trip since June 2022, once we knew he would be able to travel safely again!

So, to *Give Kids the World/Disney* we go, today! We are all excited. And to think back to one year ago, all of this still seems surreal.

The bad and the good.

It's a strange feeling, but we will be forever grateful that Ollie gets to have this experience, to feel so special and loved, at the most magical place on earth!

It's a true celebration of life. Thank you, God.

A wish kid is defined as the following: those diagnosed with critical illnesses; a progressive, degenerative, or malignant condition that has placed the child's life in jeopardy.

January 16, 2023

DAY 450.

Reflection.

We had the most incredible trip. Truly a trip of a lifetime, granted as a Wish trip to Orlando through Make-A-Wish Foundation.

The Give Kids the World Resort (GKWR) is a magical place.

The entire place is themed, with comfortable family villas, a huge splash pad/pool area, free rides, and games, including a train, a carousel, a flying bike lift, mini golf, arcade, and more!

A gift fairy that drops thoughtful gifts off each night for the wish kiddo.

There was a cafeteria with many choices for food and an ice cream shop open all day, encouraging ice cream for breakfast!

We were granted tickets to all the Disney Parks, Sea World, Universal Studios, and Legoland/Peppa Pig Land. All these tickets came with special passes we could use to either go to the front of the line or go in lightning lanes.

The speed to which we could get through rides and parks was amazing and allowed us to see so much. We walked between 16,000-20,000 steps a day. Absolutely incredible!

Ollie had the time of his life, and we were so fortunate to share the memories with Grandma and Grandpa Geen as well.

Highlights of Ollie's favorites: swimming at the resort and riding the rides at GKTW the first day; Character Meet & Greets: Mickey Mouse, twice, Minnie, Sully, Spider-Man, Captain America, Buzz Lightyear, Woody and Jessie, and Shrek.

Then there was Magic Kingdom: Seven Dwarfs Mine Train, Splash Mountain, and Peter Pan; Animal Kingdom: Kilimanjaro Safari, Na'vi River Journey, Pandora/Avatar Land; Hollywood Studios: Slinky Dog Dash, Mickey and Minnie Runaway Railway, and Rise of the Resistance from Star Wars.

And, Epcot: Frozen Ever After, Remy's Ratatouille Adventure, and Nemo.

The last day of our trip we got to see where Stellar, the Star Fairy who lives in the Castle of Miracles at GKWR, placed Ollie's miracle star. It was a very meaningful and emotional experience! There are over 200,000 stars in the Castle. It's overwhelming to see.

March 23, 2023

DAY 515 — ONE YEAR REMISSION

Yesterday, our family of three made our way to the imaging department at Cardinal Glennon at 6:15 a.m. for Ollie's one-year CT, Audiology, and labs.

He was anxious as we got him out of the house asking questions like if he had to have "tubie" or "pokies" at his visit.

We reassured him that he did not. They would be taking his blood when he was asleep under anesthesia for the scan.

We kept reiterating that this was a visit so the doctors could see how he was doing, to which he replied, "I'm good!"

Like always, I was able to hold him and walk him back to the scan room, which helps with his anxiety. We didn't do a pre-sedative this time; instead, I told him we were going to see the anesthesiologist's "office," and he was agreeable to that.

His demeanor didn't change upon entry, more curiosity than anything, and he immediately noticed Moana playing on the ceiling TV. He thought the movie was neat and said he needed to hear it better.

The doctors went through their pre-protocols, and I helped hold him and reassure him he was safe as they gave him the anesthesia.

It's still not easy to be in that space, but I know it helps him if I'm there. I leave once he is asleep and lying down on the scan table.

Brian and I went to the cafeteria to wait, had a cup of coffee, and worked. An hour later, Ollie was done, and we were being called back to recovery. He woke up within about ten minutes, and they were able to get his IV out before he messed with it.

We were able to head to Costas Center at 9:30 a.m. for our appointment. Scans, hearing test, and AFP all came back unchanged from last year!

What an incredible blessing and relief. We made it to one year.

While we are not immune to the fact that recurrence can still happen, statistics show that each year out, the less likely it is. God is good. We are eternally grateful to be where we are today. Life is so precious.

April 22, 2023

To celebrate our one-year milestone, we hosted an American Red Cross blood drive in Ollie's Honor on Saturday, April 22, 2023, from 10 a.m.–3 p.m. at the Sunset Hills Recreation Center at 3915 S. Lindbergh Saint Louis.

June 22, 2023

DAY 605

We have made it fifteen months into remission. We are beyond grateful to report that this week Ollie's quarterly scans and blood work came back unchanged!

He is in full toddler mode and loving living life.

July 17, 2023

We are once again leading Ollie's Trane Team to raise awareness and funds for Cardinal Glennon Children's Hospital. We don't have to tell this crew twice what this institution with world-class doctors and technology meant to our family! But it is our life goal to amplify awareness of what it means to us and so many.

Join us on October 15, 2023, in Forest Park in St. Louis, Missouri or participate virtually. 5k or one mile! We had an absolute blast last year and hope to continue to build on that momentum.

September 18, 2023

DAY 694: 18 MONTHS REMISSION!

A day we have been anxiously awaiting. Checkup day.

Ollie's last check was in June, and while the time in between goes very fast now, the lead-up to this day and the day itself are still intense and stressful.

In fact, we didn't tell Ollie about the visit until that morning. We don't want to cause him unnecessary anxiety.

Ollie's new protocol includes chest x-rays, ultrasound, and blood work.

First step, however, is the nothing by mouth (NPO) ahead of the imaging, which I was specifically dreading.

Ollie loves his waffle and turkey sausage when he wakes up, and doesn't understand why he can't have food or water on this random day. That's fair. Thankfully, and remarkably, he did well and only asked about it twice.

Once we got to the hospital, it was smooth sailing with imaging, Ollie even taking an interest in some of it, until the blood draw, and then the whole Costas Center heard his screaming.

I'm not so worried about the center hearing him; I just feel so bad that he is traumatized by the thought of needles. I mean, we can't blame him. It's not easy giving blood anytime, but for a small human, it's extra hard and confusing.

Thankfully, the highlights were getting to see some of our favorite people, Nurse Maddy, Dr. Lauren, Miss Bri, Ms. Charlotte, and others who are so kind and helpful.

And the news! Still all clear. Eighteen months and hopefully, God willing, forever to go. Brian and I are riding in the annual *Pedal the Cause* again this year, twenty-eight miles.

November 1, 2023

A moment of gratitude.

It's November 1, 2023; two years from the day Ollie started chemo.

It's hard to believe just how far he has come. When we started on that journey 730 days ago, we really didn't know what each day would look like, let alone two years out.

Would our boy make it?

Would he have significant hearing loss or heart damage because of the chemo regimen's potential side effects?

All we knew was we had to take each day, hour by hour, and keep our heads and hearts up and look forward. Look to the light.

Here we are. Thank God, and we do, every single day.

We enjoyed a fun-filled Halloween yesterday.

It started with a kid costume parade at his school and ended with dinner and trick-or-treating at Grandma and Grandpa Geen's.

I couldn't help but think as we were walking through the neighborhood of the kids and families up at Cardinal Glennon. It's hard to be there on a normal day, but on a holiday, especially. I remembered our Halloween spent in the hospital with Ollie.

It's not uncommon that we think of Cardinal Glennon. For those of you not local to STL, a big announcement was made last month. They are building a new Cardinal Glennon Children's Hospital. This is such exciting news for our community and reinforces my desire to stay committed long-term to helping the Foundation in any way we can.

The *Sun Run* was a tremendous success again this year! We had the largest team at 137 people and fundraised $15,560!

Between 2022–2024, our tribe has raised $50,000+ for the Cardinal Glennon Children's Foundation!

Pedal the Cause was also an amazing and fun event!

Brian and I each rode and reached our fundraising goals for Siteman Cancer Center, thank you, with the hope of a world without cancer one day. The event is so moving and meaningful, and we are very glad to have the opportunity to participate.

Pedal the Cause is one of the largest fundraising events in St. Louis, raising $3.8M this year alone to fund research projects for cancer. We can't say it enough: we feel tremendous love and support each day from our community and are truly grateful for each and every one of you.

CHAPTER 14

A NEW DAWN

November 2023:

We were back at Zadún, a Ritz-Carlton Reserve. A magical, mystical paradise at the very tip of Baja California in Cabo Del San Jose. Surrounded by Cochimís, 100+ year old cacti, and drenched in early morning sunlight, I started to feel a sense of relaxation I had not felt since our last visit, a little over one year ago. I was here to remember how to relax and, more importantly, to chase the light in the sunrises and sunsets that slow life down and help you recognize more intentionally that each day is a gift. An opportunity to start anew. Nature was so powerful in helping with that reset, both now and throughout my life, really.

It was our first morning in Mexico, and we had risen in time to watch the sunrise. With the first glimpses of sunlight on the horizon, the fishing boats that left from the nearby harbor race out for the day. Our villa had the type of retractable glass doors that you can push all the way into the wall, and the view looked like something out of a movie. Serene. Brian and I had an espresso, watching the horizon light expand to full sunlight, and then stepped out into our courtyard and onto the perfectly manicured walkway. We were surrounded by white and pink tropical flowers, delicate and lush. As I took a few steps, I noticed to my right a male cardinal.

A cardinal bird, in Mexico? In my mind, it had to be a sign. I was certainly open-minded enough to receive it. And here it was. I am fortunate to see cardinals all the time in our yard at our home in Missouri, but I genuinely didn't know they existed in Mexico. What good fortune, I thought. What did it mean, I wondered? Was it an ancestral visit of sorts, but in Mexico? We continued our walk to breakfast.

I've never felt more at peace than at Zadún. Hard to describe, but it's an overwhelming feeling of calm. Like your mind is totally free and in a Zen state, kind of like a trance. The cardinal had me thinking, and again later that morning, after we saw two lime green iguanas, what if when you die, you get to pick where your spirit goes and how you show up in the world?

I've traveled the world, and I would pick Baja California if given the choice. Maybe these animals were angel visits to us and for us? Either way, their presence intensified my feelings of experiencing magic on this property.

It reminded me of our first visit to Zadún in Fall of 2022, a year prior, almost one year exactly to the day that Ollie was diagnosed. We knew we desperately needed an energy reset after our trauma, and Zadún delivered. One day while we were sitting by the pool, which is what we did most of this vacation, one of the servers excitedly shared with us that a nest of sea turtles that had just hatched had been found on the property. As a local, he explained that this was extremely rare and exciting, and he let us know to check with the front desk on when they would be having a release ceremony. Later that day, we found out that for the turtles to have the best chance at survival, they would need to be released by the staff into the wild within a certain timeframe.

Later that evening at sunset, Brian and I were fortunate to get to experience the release of the hatchlings. It was an experience that we didn't know we would find so meaningful, especially in the context of what we had just endured with Ollie. To be honest, I had never really thought about how baby sea turtles survive. I doubt many people have. Well, that's a story in and of itself. Astonishing odds against survival, really! It is estimated that one in 1,000 hatchlings will survive to adulthood due to the many different challenges they face.

Baby sea turtles are very vulnerable. They can die from dehydration if they don't get into the ocean quickly enough. They must avoid being consumed by one of many environmental predators, such as birds, crabs, and fish, as well as avoid general human activity like fishing that could cause them to get entangled. But here we were, with the baby sea turtles being shown to us in a large Rubbermaid-type container. We were not allowed to touch them, just look. They were so very tiny. So fragile.

After everyone had a look, we were asked to step back as the naturalists carefully set the container on the ground and slowly turned it on its side. Immediately, the turtles raced towards the water.

I say "race," but this process didn't happen fast, as they were so small, but they eventually reached the water line. Some went right in, and others were pushed back aggressively by the waves. It was so interesting and poetic to observe. I stood there, memories of the past year in the hospital flooding my memory. This experience with the sea turtles was very symbolic of life and the challenges and realities that all of us face in some way or another. Eventually, after about an hour or so, most of the hatchlings had made it to the water. It was hard to realize that even those lucky enough to make it into the ocean were unlikely to survive. I have included a thank-you note from the conservation staff that we were gifted at the end of our stay. The words brought me to tears:

"Dear Mr. & Mrs. Geen:

Just like us, turtles face countless challenges throughout their life. Only those who conquer them all get to experience what a wonderful journey life is."

Death was on my mind. The Dia de Los Muertos celebrations had commenced. Visibly seeing the magnificent altars in tribute to loved ones that had passed, with their pictures and offerings, was memorable and moving.

I was so grateful to get to experience this tradition in person for once, to see it with my own eyes. I remember learning about Dia De Los Muertos in Spanish class in tenth grade at Falls High School with the fabulous Señora (Mrs. N). I was always curious about it. Celebrating the dead?

Death always seemed so sad to me based on the traditions that I had experienced in the United States. Administering of last rites, a wake, praying of the rosary with the dead body, a funeral, and then typically a burial or placement in a mausoleum if you had been cremated. All that was left to visit was a stone of some sort.Here I was looking at the most vibrant, beautiful colors of decorations. The scent of the marigolds, the unique smiling skeletons and sugar skulls, the special offerings at each picture on the altar, and their loved one's favorite human consumables, items of food and beverage.

The marigolds I was told are believed to help guide the spirits back to the world of the living. And the skeleton decor signifies that death is a part of life.

It was an absolute celebration of love and the gift of life. And when you asked a local about the annual holiday and tradition, they were eager to tell you how important it was for their family to celebrate and to honor their loved ones who had passed, to ensure that they knew they were not forgotten. It was to show those who have passed that they are forever loved and to celebrate their lives and spirits never leaving.

In writing this, I emerge out of my memory and am triggered. Ollie randomly asks about death these days, often when it's just him and me in the car. He asks questions like "Am I going to die at one hundred?" Followed with, "I don't want to die that young," adding further, "Do you get to celebrate your birthday in heaven?" I smile, I try to help him navigate human time, something we don't ever know the magic answer to. Then he asks, "What happens when we get to heaven? Do we become babies, and God helps us start again?"

It grasps me. Really. The talk of death with him. Takes my breath away. His sweet little five-year-old self, who doesn't want to die in ninety-five years, literally has no idea we came so close to death with him. Thank God for that. I also find it so perceptive of him. Although he doesn't know what death exactly means yet, somehow, he thinks about these things.

He is truly wise beyond his years.

One day, though, he will know that at the precious age of two, he fought a devastating cancer diagnosis with all his might. That he beat it, and grew to be a strong, happy, smart, and inquisitive boy. What is astonishing is that I don't think he will directly remember any of it. Not the pain, not the suffering that he went through at that time. For that, I am eternally grateful. This experience did not break his spirit.

The experience I faced with Ollie really made me lean back into faith over fear, despite knowing that death could be an outcome. It didn't break my spirit either. It made me reevaluate life and how I was living each day.

Throughout this journey, I did fear the worst but also knew that if the worst happened, God would be with me, as he was with me when my mom passed away. In my late teens and early twenties, I often asked God why I endured the pain of losing my mom so young. I tried to reason with it for years. Like, why, just why, couldn't she still be here? She is missed so very much, and she has missed so much, not only with me but with my siblings as well. I then resolved in my twenties that I would never know the answer. God will, but I won't. I had to be okay with that.

And when we were going through Ollie's ordeal, I asked "why" again. As if this time, I would have an answer. There are no answers to these things. They just are. Lean into all of it. The pain, the sorrow, the grief, the anxiety, and the lessons learned in the space between.

I urge you to take the time you are given on this earth to appreciate all that is and all that can be in your life.

You might have one hundred years. You might have two. You might have fifty-some, like my mom.

At age forty, I find myself contemplating the concept of time more than ever. Especially in the context of, "What if I only have forty good years left?" Alternatively, I should think to myself, "I would be so lucky to have forty good years left." We always think we have more time.

We always think the bad things are not going to happen to us or our loved ones.

Remember that even one hundred years on this planet is short. Time is our most precious resource and one we spend without ever knowing how much of it is left. It is my sincere hope that in sharing Ollie's story you can see how choosing to find the light and stand in it can illuminate and help shift your perspective during difficult and trying times.

THE SUNRISE

December 17, 2024

It has been three short and long years since we were in a lifeboat in the middle of the storm; what I would categorize felt to me like a category four hurricane. I can still hear it, see it, feel it. It came on quick. We almost didn't have time to take cover, to prepare before it ripped through all we knew of our lives. We braced for the worst and took wave after wave with gusty winds before we were able to resurface to step outside and feel the sun on our skin.

It was awful.

Childhood cancer in the middle of an ongoing global pandemic.

As you might imagine, it is still very difficult to mentally put myself back into the details of the experience we lived. To recall it. To sit in it. To feel it. It was traumatic.

With time, I have paused and let myself take the emotional waves as they come with re-reading the CaringBridge Journals, recalling and reliving the many moments and memories.

The panic, the devastation, the disbelief, the hope, the faith, the joy, the love, and the light.

The absolute miracle of it all.

We still live with fear of a potential relapse or secondary cancer finding. We still worry about long-lasting and damaging effects of the intense and toxic chemo protocol.

All of that is still there, right below the surface. It rises infrequently, but especially when we are in the actual hospital for follow-up appointments. Like when we walk the hallway to the Dallas Heart Center and hold Ollie's hand as he has an ECHO screening and EKG, while we watch quietly and patiently the technician complete an ultrasound of his liver in that dark, quiet room in the Imaging Department. Steps retraced from when we lived at Cardinal Glennon.

One of the most poignant things that will sit with my heart forever is the overwhelming lift from our community.

When I say community, I mean friends and family, and then those who knew our friends and family, and those who didn't know us at all. I mean community organizations like Friends of Kids with Cancer, Basket of Hope, Children's Miracle Network, and many others. It was quite remarkable just how many people cared. How many people prayed, sent us meals, messages, and gifts.

Ollie's journey is an unbelievable story. But it's real. One that I lived, my husband lived, and my son endured. One that many who knew us, and many who didn't, lived alongside us and helped us live by lifting us in love.

Oliver's story shocks and surprises people to this day. Looking at him, you would never know or guess what this child has gone through. That he is a childhood cancer survivor. Whenever I share this fact about Ollie, people are shocked. Stunned. I see it in their face. I get so many questions. How did we find out? What type of treatment did he receive? How did we manage? What now? That is in part why I wrote this book.

Oliver represents many things about life. How short life can be. How life can change in a moment. How circumstances are not always fair or easy. How resilience can be achieved even in the worst of circumstances. How hope can be small but mighty, and how light can always shine in the darkness. That is something he taught me.

Each day since Ollie's bell-ringing ceremony has been a "re-birth" of sorts. I know that may sound dramatic, but it's true for Brian, Ollie, and me, each in different ways.

A "re-building," a "re-calibration" as I told friend Meredith, who herself recently beat stage-4 lymphoma. There is no "going back" to how or who you were before.

Not mentally. Not emotionally. Not physically.

You have to choose to rebuild and recalibrate yourself from such a life experience. That is the beauty in it, if you choose to see it that way.

And while Ollie's story is unique, each one of us will likely go through a difficult, painful, unexpected "that wasn't on my bingo card for life" moment, or many such moments.

Maybe repeatedly.

Maybe unfairly.

Always untimely.

The point is, you can choose to keep seeing the light in it all. Both sadness and joy, <u>and</u> darkness and light, <u>and</u> faith and doubt, and happiness and sadness, can all co-exist.

Only you can save your mind from the dark places it will go to under these circumstances. And that includes knowing when you need to get help. Help is available in such a variety of ways, but you need to allow yourself to be open to receiving it.

In addition to the anti-anxiety medication, finding time for fitness like my Orangetheory Classes or running was very important to my mental endurance. Sometimes just taking a simple and slow walk to the mailbox, writing thank you notes, seeing a bird, or a cloud, or the bright moon at night, the sunset or sunrise, helped. It could be a few one-minute moments that I cobbled together throughout the day that kept me thinking there is more to this planet than the pain I am enduring. I will never forget that day that I spoke of in the Caring-Bridge Journals when I saw a bumper sticker that said, "Hope Wins." It made me smile, think, acknowledge the opportunity for hope, and recognize that I indeed was looking for it.

Signs are everywhere when you look.

Ollie has reached three years of remission and now goes in quarterly to Cardinal Glennon for blood tests and ultrasounds.

These appointments have gotten easier for the most part, but our six-year-old absolutely hates getting his blood drawn. I can't blame him. As such, we must hold him on our laps with his arms tucked underneath ours so he doesn't run or move his arm, and remind him through his tears and anxiety that it will be quick. "Why do I have to?" he asks. We try to explain that the doctors still need to look at his blood to make sure he is healthy. A strange conversation with a child.

We always get the reply, "But I feel great! My belly is all better!"

Ollie started kindergarten this year at our local parish school, Saint Catherine Laboure, and it has been amazing and unique to see him learn and grow, make new friends, be active in sports; swimming, soccer, and basketball, and expand his faith and relationship with God.

Each year, one special project the kindergarten class does on or around Dia de Los Muertos (All Saints day) is to pick a patron saint to be. They dress up like this saint and learn some facts about their life, and then they have a "Saint day." We guided Ollie to pick Saint Peregrine, the patron saint of those suffering from cancer.

The Saint day presentation was a full-circle moment for me. Almost out of body.

The kindergarten saints' parade in through the front doors of the sanctuary with full costume on and proceed down the center aisle. They are singing "When the Saints Go Marching In." They take a seat in the wooden pews and one by one go up to the front of the dais and say their bit into the microphone. It was finally Ollie's turn. In the silence of the church, my five-year-old son walked up to the microphone.

"Hi, I'm Ollie Geen, and my patron saint is Saint Peregrine." I watched in pure anticipation and joy. "I am the patron saint of those suffering from cancer. I am a model for those suffering from sickness. My feast day is May 1."

Cheers and clapping erupted.

Yes, my boy, you are a model, for me and so many. Now, forever and always.

It was a surreal, powerful, memorable, and joyful reminder.

"Light" to me comes in many different forms:

Through prayer

Through humans/community

Through yoga & meditation

Through nature, especially sunlight/moonlight/stars

Through music

Through movement

Through literature

Through animals

Through creative outlets

Through photos

Through daydreaming

Through cooking

Through writing

ACKNOWLEDGMENTS

Thank you for taking the time to read the story of Oliver Geen. Writing this book brought a lot of light into my life throughout the multi-year process. My hope is that Ollie's story can somehow provide encouragement to find small moments to always chase the light and live, whatever that means to you.

I want to thank all the people who helped us endure Ollie's diagnosis and treatment. First and foremost, the doctors, nurses, and professional staff at Cardinal Glennon Children's Hospital and Saint Louis Children's Hospital, you all are the definition of heroes. A very special thank you to NP Jenny, Dr. Lauren, and Dr. Baddr. I'd like to acknowledge and especially thank my in-laws, Brian's parents, Jerry and Anna Geen. Our family, specifically our siblings, nieces, nephews, cousins, and aunts and uncles. Our nanny Miss Kaitlin. Our friends, especially my friends in Missouri City/County Management Association (MCMA), the Local Government Gals (LGGs), Orangetheory Fitness (OTF), and Wine Group. Our employers, our neighbors, Ollie's daycare, Lakeside Children's Academy, and the many community organizations, such as Friends of Kids with Cancer and Basket of Hope. I'd also like to thank those who encouraged me to write this book, specifically Tammy-Jo, Lauren, and my cousin/professional writer Allana, who helped me finalize and edit this manuscript. And lastly, I'd like to thank my husband Brian for being a strong and steadfast partner to me and an amazing father to Oliver.

COMMITMENT

Half of any proceeds made from the sale of this book will be donated on an annual basis to the Cardinal Glennon Children's Foundation, in perpetuity.

Cardinal Glennon Children's Hospital is located in St. Louis, Missouri, and was instrumental in saving Ollie's life. With this experience, I have been called to be an ambassador for the organization in helping to amplify the lifesaving work that is done there.

Cardinal Glennon Children's Hospital's mission is:

"Since opening our doors in 1956 as the nation's first freestanding Catholic children's hospital, SSM Health Cardinal Glennon has remained steadfast in our commitment to exceptional and accessible health care. Over the years, we have proudly served over 10 million children in need from the bi-state region of Missouri and Illinois and beyond. Our devotion has never been stronger, and the need has never been greater. At Cardinal Glennon, we ensure our doors are always open for a child in need, as we are more than just a hospital, we are a devoted partner in the health and well-being of families. Many of our programs and services thrive through the generosity of friends, partners, and donors as we live our mission every day: Through our exceptional health care services, we reveal the healing presence of God."

SSM Health Cardinal Glennon Children's Foundation's mission is:

"SSM Health Cardinal Glennon Children's Foundation, led by our Board of Governors, provides the financial support necessary for delivering exceptional healthcare, in state-of-the-art facilities, to all children in need of care. Through pro-active communication efforts, community cultivation, philanthropic generosity and Christ-like stewardship, the Foundation's purpose is to build strong partnerships that will result in world-class pediatric health care at SSM Health Cardinal Glennon Children's Hospital."

ABOUT THE AUTHOR

Jennifer (Gray) Geen grew up in rural Northern Minnesota in International Falls, a town nicknamed the "Icebox of the Nation." After graduating from Falls High School, she moved to Missouri to pursue her college education. She holds a Bachelor of Science Degree in History from Lincoln University and a Master of Arts Degree in Public Administration from Saint Louis University.

Jennifer is the Founder of Graylight Collective LLC, a holding company for various types of creative works with a mission for lifting and amplifying light in people, places, and communities across the globe. She and her husband Brian, son Oliver, and golden-doodle Bella live in a suburban community in St. Louis County, Missouri.